YOUR BEST YEAR YET

Weekly Personal Growth Challenges to **Unlock Your Best Self**

Linda Kneidinger, MS, MEd
Founder, Ultimate You Coaching

ISBN: 979-8-9918387-0-2
eISBN: 979-8-9918387-1-9

Book Cover Design and Interior Formatting by 100Covers.

"Life isn't about finding yourself. Life is about creating yourself."

~ George Bernard Shaw

CONTENTS

PREFACE

AS A LIFE and health coach, I'm always exploring new methods for getting helpful information into the hands of people who seek it. In addition to one-on-one work with clients, I speak to organizations, partner with sports teams, run workshops, and share quotes and inspirational tidbits on social media.

Still, I'd been feeling that there had to be a better way to reach more people who desired strategies that could help them change their lives.

For a long time (although I wouldn't admit it to myself), what I *really* wanted to do was publish a book. The obstacle in my way, however, was me. I didn't consider myself a "writer." Didn't writers major in English, journalism, or communication?

When I came across Regina Brett's quote, "A writer writes. If you want to be a writer, write," I had an idea. What if I honed my writing by creating a weekly newsletter?

Many coaches complain that the reason they don't post on social media is that they can't think of topics to write about. That has *never* been my problem! I have long lists of topics all over the place! In the Notes app on my phone, in emails to myself, on scraps of paper and sticky notes on my desk, in my purse, and in my tote bag.

I knew I had plenty to share, but was my writing good enough to attract—and retain—subscribers? And did I have the discipline to write a newsletter EVERY WEEK?

I'm proud to say I'm now several years into my weekly newsletter and haven't missed a week. I also haven't reused any old newsletters. I come up with something fresh every week.

What I'm most proud of, though, is the connection I've created with my readers. Not only have I built a significant subscriber list with an open rate that's regularly around 70% (17% is average, and 30% is considered good), but every week, people take the time to respond to my emails and let me know how they used what they learned. I can't express what that means to me!

After proving to myself that I'm a decent enough writer with some useful information to share, I took the plunge and started writing a book. (Spoiler alert—this isn't the book I started with!)

When I can keep my butt in a chair and focus, the words come easily. But when a block of time for writing comes up in my calendar, it often takes mental gymnastics to psych myself up and calm myself down so I can sit still and do the work of writing. For some reason, even though I knew a newsletter was doable, planning to tackle a book, even a small chunk of a book, is more daunting.

After finishing 90% of the work, I began to drag my feet. I needed a break, but I didn't want to lose momentum toward my goal of publishing a book. I remembered a marketing workshop I once attended that taught the importance of recycling your work. While I've never republished the same newsletter to my email list, I realized I had a mountain of writing already done that could easily become my first book!

It was inspiring to go back and read my old newsletters, and it did seem a shame that they had only been shared once. It took a year to reconfigure these nuggets into a cohesive narrative, but I love the finished product. I hope you do, too.

Now that *this* book is finished, it's time to get back to work on my original book. I'm close to being done, and having proven to myself that I can tackle this challenge has increased my confidence, focus, energy, and motivation.

My writing journey is an example of how I walk the talk when it comes to using effective strategies to accomplish goals. I gave myself a break when I hit a wall, but I didn't run away or quit. I found an opportunity for an easy win. I reminded myself of my gifts, passion, and purpose. I got myself an accountability partner to help me stay on task.

If you give yourself these 52 opportunities to shift your perspectives, mindsets, and beliefs, and you complete the actions that can lead to new habits, you'll also end up with a mountain of successes!

I hope you dig in and hold yourself accountable to completing this whole book. I want this for you! My love, support, and encouragement alone can't make it happen for you, though. For change to happen, you must *do the work*. Knowing what you want and why are just the first steps. But please know that I'm here cheering you on!

You deserve to show up in your life as your best self. These 52 strategies and actions will help you access and honor your best self. When you peel away the layers and let your authentic self shine, you'll gain peace in your soul that will guide you through anything life throws your way.

INTRODUCTION

52 weeks. One year. A lot can happen in one year. Conversely, absolutely nothing can happen in one year. A year is absolutely what you make of it.

Big, dramatic events make it easier to create change in your life. These might include family changes like parenthood or becoming an empty nester, the illness or death of a loved one, mental or physical health challenges, relationship shifts such as marriage, infidelity, separation, or divorce, career changes like relocation, job change, or retirement, or simply hitting rock bottom.

With such events, our lives naturally shift, whether we want them to or not. We can take the wheel and steer the direction of the shift or passively accept where life takes us.

It's a lot harder, however, to create change in your life when things are mostly okay. Change requires energy, and our brains are designed to monitor our energy investments carefully. They're also designed to interpret change as risky. So, when things are good—or even just not terrible—change requires us to battle our brains and win.

As a life coach with a background in neuroscience and psychology, I use the science of how people think (cognitive psychology) to help clients successfully create change in their lives. I've been a total brain geek since high school, when an experience as an athlete got me curious about the connection between thoughts, actions, and the outcomes in our lives.

In my coaching, most clients haven't had the benefit of big, dramatic events thrusting them into change. Most were doing pretty well in their lives but knew they were capable of more. Some felt a little unsettled and wanted to face what they were avoiding. They recognized that they needed new mindsets and beliefs and an accountability partner to get things going.

I've helped people through tough decisions, such as returning to school later in life, changing jobs, and shifting relationships. I've been with them as they changed habits that led to losing weight, reclaiming time, and quitting smoking. I've helped them show up more powerfully in their lives by setting boundaries, improving communication, and reconnecting with their authentic selves.

To get these results, you often need to overcome obstacles such as perfectionism, procrastination, self-doubt, imposter syndrome, people-pleasing, fear of failure, and insecurity. As you'll discover in this book, all of these struggles are normal, and their origins make sense, but they get in the way of us achieving what we desire.

Whatever YOUR specific reason, something drove you to pick up this book. You recognized that with a little help, you could live a brighter, happier, more satisfying life. This book will make it easy to take meaningful steps toward that goal.

The structure of this book is the same as the newsletters I send my clients. Each week, I'll introduce a topic, explain how it impacts our lives, and offer action-step "challenges" to help you implement these concepts in real life.

You may read this book as fast or slow as you'd like, but ideally, you'll read *one entry* each week. That gives you seven days to try each challenge, which is enough time for some practice but not so much time that you'll forget or have time to procrastinate.

And, by doing one challenge per week, you'll build momentum and begin to create shifts you'll start feeling and seeing. You need *consistency* for new beliefs, attitudes, and habits to take hold.

Please make notes on the lined pages following each entry! It's important to capture your initial thoughts about each topic and challenge. Writing down your thoughts and plans helps cement them in memory and increases your chance of follow-through. It also turns this book into a journal of sorts, capturing where you were in your life when you read it.

Even if you decide the challenge is dumb or irrelevant to you, note that. When you're further into the year, you might reflect differently on a topic and find your initial impression revealing.

If you stick to it and create the habit of reading and actioning on *one* short entry each week, you'll be creating the building blocks for success. Consistency is built into the structure of this book.

Learning about human behavior alone won't shift how you show up in the world. You need to reflect on how you're showing up now and then *try* something different. That's what I love about coaching—the focus is on *taking action* based on personal awareness and a widened view of what's possible.

The shifts you'll create through this book are easy because, individually, they're small. No matter how big the change you desire in your life, the most effective way to achieve it is always a journey of small, consistent steps.

Even if you get off track, if this book ends up at the bottom of the books stacked on your nightstand, don't quit! Put notes on your calendar to remind yourself to find the book and keep going!

Bookmark the challenges that resonate with you most deeply, are hardest for you, or make no sense. Come back later and do them again. Or keep revisiting the entire book! Growth can pass through the same lesson over and over and take you to a new level every time.

If you keep reading the entries and trying the simple challenges, you *can* create massive changes in your life. If you're consistent, you'll have new habits and perspectives by the end of one year. As I said, a lot can happen in a year. Or nothing can happen. The choice is yours.

If you're ready to learn, reflect, and act, read on! Take the wheel and steer yourself on a journey of personal growth—a journey to your ultimate you!

Get to know your inner Anxious Mouse

LET'S KICK OFF this year of personal growth with one of my favorite topics—the voice in your head. Everyone has one, and everyone's chatter is nonstop.

The chatter itself isn't the problem. The problem is that this voice is often negative. It tries to talk you out of things, points out the dangers and pitfalls in your ideas and plans, and says, "I told you so," when things go badly.

I mentioned in the introduction that an experience as a high school athlete was what first got me interested in the power of our thoughts. It was this **inner voice** that I was curious about.

I was my team's number-one singles player, but I wasn't a "country club" player. I was an above-average athlete with decent tennis skills. I could hold my own against most people, but I was in over my head against many other number-one players.

Once, during a match, my coach told me I wasn't "concentrating" enough. At the time, I didn't know anything about sports psychology (and this was the 80s before it was mainstream), but what I DID know was that it seemed the more I intentionally focused on my play, the worse I played.

You'll encounter lots of topics in this book that could have helped me create more productive thinking habits back then. What I now understand is that when matches got tight, my self-talk went negative, and when my self-talk went negative, my play got worse. I didn't know how to fix this, so the cycle continued and my frustration grew.

Most people think they're the only ones who have this problem. If everyone else out there is achieving, succeeding, and being brave, something must be broken in *us* if *our* brain doesn't think we're as capable as everyone else.

But negative self-talk is normal, and it turns out it has a productive function—it *thinks* it's protecting us. Without this voice, we might do *truly* dangerous things that would regularly put our lives at risk.

Losing our lives is *definitely* not in our best interest, so it's a good thing our brain keeps an eye on us. But in modern life, there are very few scenarios in our day-to-day existence that *actually* threaten our lives.

Unfortunately, our brain doesn't recognize the difference between losing a tennis match and wandering into a lion's den. It sees danger where the worst possible outcome might be disappointment or discomfort.

Since we can't turn off this voice, we need to monitor it so it doesn't go rogue. We need to respect its function while reality-testing its concerns.

The two most common ways of dealing with this voice are ineffective. **Ignoring** it is like trying to push a beach ball underwater—the harder you push, the harder it resists.

Attacking this voice doesn't work either. This voice is *part* of you, but it doesn't represent *all* of you. Treating yourself unkindly *never* leads to happiness and growth.

My most popular mental hack is the strategy I've developed for managing this voice. I've taught this approach to children, teens, adults, men, women, and, to come full circle, athletes. *Everyone* I've taught it to loves this strategy. And

I call it the **Anxious Mouse Method.**

People *love* the Anxious Mouse Method because it's memorable, relatable, compassionate, and effective. I've given many talks about this method, so it's not uncommon for people to see me in public and say, "Hey! I know you, you're the Anxious Mouse lady!"

Anxious Mouse represents the voice inside your head. I have a cute little felt mouse with a scarf and an adorable face that I share with clients and during presentations. He's always greeted with an audible *"Awwww!"*

Anxious Mouse means well, but he's just a sweet little mouse with a tiny mouse brain. He doesn't understand modern human life; he only knows *survival*. Anything he thinks might jeopardize your survival will set him off on a spree of *anxious squeaking* in your head.

If he thought the only threats to your safety were big animals and dangerous environments, he'd be easy to deal with. But he *also* believes there's safety in numbers, so he doesn't want you to lose face in your pack. That means anything that might jeopardize your acceptance by others will set him off.

His fearful squeaking gets triggered by the thought of failing, being laughed at, standing out, appearing weak, being wrong, seeming stupid, making people angry, and hurting people's feelings.

Anxious Mouse is why we say yes when we want to say no, dumb ourselves down, avoid challenges we might fail at, go along with the group, and withhold our feelings.

The most effective way to handle Anxious Mouse is to use my Anxious Mouse Method:

1. When you notice him anxiously squeaking in your head, take a moment to acknowledge that your situation has activated your Anxious Mouse.

2. Listen to him without *believing* him. His message is always based on your individual experience—your fears and insecurities—so there's value in knowing what situations feel unsafe to *your* Anxious Mouse.

3. Thank him for caring!!! He is part of you, and treating him with gratitude and compassion is the same as treating *yourself* with gratitude and compassion. He's trying to keep you safe. He's just a misguided little mouse.

4. Assure him that you have the situation under control, and then send him off to his burrow for a nap. Then, use your big, smart, human brain to think through the *reality* of the situation so you can *consciously* make choices that serve you.

HERE'S YOUR CHALLENGE FOR THE WEEK

Self-talk is constant. You literally can't make it stop. Scientists can "see" this with fMRIs when they tell subjects to try not to think of anything. So, let's begin by becoming aware of what we say to ourselves. That's where we *do* have control.

When you notice your thoughts going off on their own, stop and listen to them with a bit of detachment. Is this your Anxious Mouse speaking to you? If so, go through the four steps of the **Anxious Mouse Method**.

After you've done this a few times, you'll begin to get an idea of the types of situations that trigger the squeaking for you. Then you can ask yourself:

- What do these situations have in common?

- Why does your Anxious Mouse label these situations as dangerous?

- What fears might be connected to the things your Anxious Mouse labels as danger?

- Where in your life might these fears have come from?

Consider some positive, true statements you can call on when Anxious Mouse tries to protect you. Something like, "I've made it through tough times before, and I have the skills to do it again." Or "I'm doing my best, and other people's judgments about me are not my concern."

Anxious Mouse will always try to hold you back in the name of "safety;" it's his job. It's up to *you* to decide whether his fears represent *real* dangers or just the possibility of discomfort.

I'm sure you can withstand a little discomfort in the name of personal growth and fulfillment! I witness people successfully do hard things all the time. The payoff is worth the pain.

The status quo is comfortable until it starts to feel like stagnation. Experiencing life with joy and inner peace involves growing and changing.

Give the **Anxious Mouse Method** a try this week. It's the first step in your year of growth and change. We'll build on this in the coming weeks, but if you're pushing yourself out of your comfort zone, your Anxious Mouse *will* come up again and again. Getting acquainted with him and learning to manage him will be a crucial part of creating something extraordinary over the next year.

You've got this! See you next week!

NOTES

....

....

....

....

....

....

....

....

....

....

....

....

....

....

....

Pick one goal to start working on

IT'S *WEEK TWO* of your year of personal growth. Past failures to create the life you desire are wiped from your mind, and you're sure that using this book will help you finally get where you want to go. *Right?*

I hate to be a downer, but it's not that easy. Yes, hope and optimism are absolutely essential to creating change in your life. They're what keep you going during the tough times. Hope without action leads to disappointment, however. *Action* is the magic ingredient in creating change!

Action can be scary and intimidating, though. The work can seem too hard; the road can seem too long. Sometimes, you don't even know where to start or what actions to take.

For me, *wanting* to write a book was easy. *Imagining* writing a book was fun. Scheduling time in my calendar for writing was a simple first step. But the *action* of sitting and writing a whole book was intimidating and hard, which is why so many people who have this dream let it die.

Fear and a lack of knowledge about where to start are both normal reactions to change. That's why this week, we're going to break down the obstacles to your goal so it doesn't become an unrealized dream.

You don't need to know the whole path to your destination when you begin the journey. You just need to know *what* your goal is and *why* it's important to you. Let's figure out those two things, then this week's challenge will take it from there.

Take a minute to dream about what you'd like the next 52 weeks to look like. Close your eyes and imagine a life that would make you happy. Imagine goals reached, relationships improved, and skills built. Maybe you desire less busyness, a different job, better nutrition, or more daily physical movement.

Marinate in this vision. Get specific. Engage your senses. Run through a whole day, a month, a season, or the whole year in your mind.

Where are you? Who are you with? What's happening? How does this imaginary life differ from how you're living right now? How does it make you *feel*?

When you're done with this visualization, write down what stood out to you. Notice I didn't say type it. Writing with your hand activates different parts of your brain than typing. Writing down your thoughts is a powerful way to seal in the benefits for all the challenges in this book.

Then...

HERE'S YOUR CHALLENGE FOR THE WEEK

Pick *one* thing from this vision that feels good and is making a big impact on how "future you" is living. Something that feels important and exciting, something that would be a shame for you *not* to have in your life.

Write down this dream for yourself. This is big! You might have never admitted to yourself that you desire this thing. Congratulate yourself for your bravery, honesty, and willingness to engage in vulnerable self-discovery.

Next, think backward about the steps that might have led you from where you are now to this wonderful, imaginary new reality. Then, decide what the very first, itty-bitty, teeny-tiny, bite-sized action is that you can take *this week* to get this journey started.

I'm talking *small*! Something there's absolutely no reason you wouldn't be able to accomplish in a week. It might be a web search or a phone call. You might need to learn a fact, buy materials, or put a reminder of a new habit in your environment where you'll see it every day. Maybe you need to speak it into the universe and share your dream with someone you trust.

Now, put this action item on your calendar! Decide *exactly* when you'll do it. Put sticky note reminders in your environment to make sure you don't forget. Doing this *one* thing puts you on the path to change.

Little changes snowball into big changes. One little not-so-hard task becomes part of another bigger task that's a little easier, which makes up a bigger task, and so on. I've seen this happen repeatedly with my clients. I know it's true!

If you *don't* complete that first step this week, ask yourself what got in the way. What kept you from taking an action that serves your own goals, wants, and dreams?

Inaction can provide valuable information. What do you fear? What might you have to give up to get the good thing you desire? Why do you value that *so much* that you'll let it be an obstacle to your dream?

If you make it a habit to mindfully reflect on *why* you do the things you do, your introspection and self-discovery will help you make better decisions for the rest of your life. This single habit can be a game-changer.

So, this week, take your first step, then identify the next one, and the next one, and so on. If you're consistent and hold yourself accountable, you'll have achieved something amazing by the time you finish this book. You also will have taught yourself that you have the ability to make your dreams a reality.

You've got this! See you next week.

NOTES

....

....

....

....

....

....

....

....

....

....

....

....

....

....

....

....

WEEK 3

Create a mindset that supports your goals

I'VE BEEN A runner since junior high. I'm one of those weirdos who loves running. To preserve my joints, I do most of my "running" on an elliptical now. I love the energy, community, and competition at road races, though, so I try to register for a 10K every month.

I do well for my age group, usually placing in the top three at smaller, local races. Shortly before writing this book, I had a particularly successful 10K experience where I finished first in my age group and 25th out of 175 runners.

During the race, as I glided by runners half my age, I knew I had an unfair advantage over them. I take my physical health seriously, doing some type of workout at least five days a week, but most people at a 10K are in pretty good shape. *I* knew it was my *mental game* that was giving me an edge.

As we discussed earlier when I introduced you to Anxious Mouse, our brains *never* turn off their commentary about what's going on in our lives. And, no matter what you're doing, the brain's natural inclination is to think negatively. This is called the **Negativity Bias**. If you don't have a strong mental game, you'll let your brain talk you out of things that are important to you or convince you that you can't do things you're fully capable of.

I learned this the hard way through the high school tennis experience I shared with you earlier.

It's taken me a long time and a lot of practice—and it does require *practice*—but now I have an answer for anything my brain serves up. I'm never harsh with myself—I always treat these negative thoughts with tenderness and compassion—but I don't let them win.

Let me walk you through what this looks like for me during a 10K, and then we'll set your challenge for this week.

The most common thought that pops into my mind when running is, *"I'm tired. Let's walk."* While there's nothing wrong with walking, if my intention had been to run the entire distance (and win my age group), I analyze this thought before giving in to it.

How tired *am* I? Have I been this tired before and kept going anyway? If so, what happened? How about I keep going for five more minutes and then reassess how I feel? If I still feel tired after five more minutes of running, I could slow down for a while and see if that's what I need to replenish my energy.

This process is similar to my Anxious Mouse strategy: listen to the thought, compassionately challenge it, and then mindfully and intentionally choose the next action.

The brain can be like a toddler. If you have children or have ever dealt with toddlers, you know they can react impulsively. Their initial reaction to a situation is rarely the result of critical thinking.

When I'm (compassionately) challenging my thoughts, I treat my brain like I'm dealing with a toddler. I seek to understand *why* it says what it does, but I question those thoughts so I can keep forging ahead toward my goal!

HERE'S YOUR CHALLENGE FOR THE WEEK

Let's get you out of your comfort zone! And let's do it with a compassionate strategy rather than brute force or self-attack.

This week, try something that feels a little scary. Take that first step. Most things in life aren't black and white. In my example, I could have chosen to walk after five more minutes of running if it turned out I really was out of energy. I just didn't need to take that action immediately.

What does *your* brain try to talk you out of? Tough challenges? Uncomfortable conversations? Setting and communicating boundaries? Saying no? Trying new experiences? Risking failure?

Listen to your brain's message as if it's coming from a toddler. Have compassion for that scared toddler. Understand why it might say what it's saying. But *don't give in!*

Use your logical, rational brain to respond. Push yourself to stay in the discomfort a little longer than usual and give yourself reasonable criteria for when you'll back off and create a new, less stressful strategy.

During my 10K, after I ran for five more minutes, the desire to walk was gone! My brain had moved on. I felt fine, and the urge to quit running had passed. By that time, I had made it to the top of a long incline, where I was greeted with a gorgeous view of the ocean. I felt a surge of energy that inspired me to increase my speed on the way back down. Thank goodness I hadn't given in right away!

One of the most significant skills I help clients develop is the ability to manage their inner dialogue. This isn't just a skill that is valuable in sports; it's a skill for *life.*

No matter what you're trying to achieve, you can either be the greatest threat to your success or your own best cheerleader. Your thoughts can support moving ahead or staying put. Producing productive thoughts is a *skill.* Practice this skill, and you'll be amazed at what you can accomplish.

You've got this! See you next week.

NOTES

....

....

....

....

....

....

....

....

....

....

....

....

....

....

....

....

....

Tune into your inner truth

WHEN SOMETHING UNCOMFORTABLE happens in your life, do you ever feel sick to your stomach? Do you get headaches when there's tension and anxiety in your life? Does your dentist look at your molars and ask if you ever clench your jaw? (The last one's a little personal!)

Our emotions don't just live in our heads; they live in our bodies, too. Have you ever reflected on something emotional from your past—good or bad—and physically felt the same way you felt when the event originally happened? Try it right now.

Your body is a much more reliable reporter than your brain when determining how something makes you feel. We can self-edit in our brain, convincing ourselves that something doesn't really bother us when it does. We can talk ourselves out of fully experiencing good feelings, too.

But our body doesn't hold back. It doesn't know how to lie, diminish, protect, or defend. Neurotransmitters get released, and our body reacts. It's that simple.

This is important because often we've lied to ourselves *so many times* about how we feel that we don't even know the truth anymore. I see this all the time with my clients.

They'll say it doesn't bother them that they've grown distant from their spouse or didn't get the promotion *again*. They'll say they don't mind always being the one to compromise with friends.

But by paying attention to their voice and body language, I can tell they're not speaking their truth, even when they insist they are.

If you settle in your seat, slow your breath, and turn your attention inward, you can begin to *feel* your truth. It seems backward for your body to tell your brain how you feel, but it works.

HERE'S YOUR CHALLENGE FOR THE WEEK

Practice taking time to listen to your body in all kinds of situations. Stop and check in with your inner state. Get reacquainted with your **body wisdom**.

In moments where you feel happy, sad, tense, rushed, relaxed, angry, loved, ignored—all the feelings—scan your body to see how these emotions might be expressing themselves in your physical body.

You can do the reverse as well. When you're not sure *how* you're feeling, take a moment to do a body scan. Is there an energy or a tension somewhere? This is a sign that you're holding a feeling in your body. Note *how* your body holds this feeling and run through some **emotion words** to identify what it might be.

(We'll talk about this in greater depth later, but search online for an "**emotion wheel**" to help you expand your emotional vocabulary.)

Notice when your body and mind aren't aligned. Why might your mind want to protect you from what you're feeling? Is it a scary thing to admit to yourself? Are you afraid it might become too overwhelming?

If it was unacceptable to feel or express certain emotions as a child ("boys don't cry" is a common seed of self-rejection), the feeling in your body and your emotion may have become disconnected. You might look externally for the source of your discomfort rather than explore your feelings.

We can struggle to let in the good as much as we avoid the bad. Sadly, it's common to think we're unworthy of overwhelming happiness or to be able to acknowledge our blessings if we're committed to a victim identity.

Breathe into what your body is telling you. This is your **inner truth**. Rejecting it is self-rejection, which leads to inner tension.

Greet yourself where you are, with all the feelings that come with being human. Bringing your body and mind into alignment is your gift to yourself this week.

You've got this! See you next week.

NOTES

....

....

....

....

....

....

....

....

....

....

....

....

....

....

....

....

Free yourself from obsessive thoughts

DOES THIS EVER happen to you? Something doesn't go your way, or you wish you'd handled a situation differently, or someone ticks you off, and the scenario replays in your mind *over* and *over* and *over* again.

It happened to me recently when I was weeding a flower bed. (Time spent weeding is a great opportunity for mind-wandering.)

As brains tend to do, my mind wandered into *negative* territory. I needed to set some boundaries with one of my clients who consistently rescheduled appointments, and I slipped into obsessing over how I'd been enabling this behavior.

It's easy to get wrapped up in these types of thoughts. Our brains are meaning-making machines, so when something doesn't make sense or activates our Anxious Mouse, we can burn up incredible amounts of mental energy replaying the scenario.

Here's the thing, though—these endless thought loops are rarely productive. They waste our time and hijack our minds, leaving us feeling agitated or upset, but they *don't* lead to insights, revelations, or solutions.

Given what we've covered so far, you won't be surprised to learn that we're predisposed to latch onto negative thoughts. We're wired to focus on things that have, or could, cause us harm. What a shame to live with a mind that's stuck rehashing the worst parts of our experience!

Luckily, there's a way to keep yourself from getting locked in these obsessive thought loops so your mind and mood can stay productive and positive.

First, you need to catch yourself. This is the first step for a lot of my strategies. Changing your thinking requires becoming *aware* of your thinking. When you get in the habit of observing your thoughts, you'll get good at detecting when they've drifted off in a direction that doesn't serve you.

Next, once you've noticed you're stuck on something, you have a decision to make.

If the situation requires *action*—either correcting something that already happened or making sure it doesn't happen again—decide what action you'd like to take, what your very first step should be, and make a plan for *taking* that first step.

If you're just stuck *replaying* an incident or thought from the past, it's time to try the practice of **non-attachment**. In its simplest form, non-attachment means letting things go.

With non-attachment (we'll get into this more later), we accept that a feeling or thought exists, but we don't latch onto it. We let it come into our awareness and then pass right on by. We let go of our impulse to enter into conversation with every wandering thought that enters our mind.

I often use the analogy of clouds floating by on a windy day with my clients. We acknowledge each cloud that comes into our sight and allow it to pass by. It was here, and now it's gone. Once it has passed, we don't chase after it.

If you have trouble letting go of a thought, your senses can help you anchor in the present. Play a game with yourself, such as naming five things you see and hear. Or focus on one sense at a time. Pay attention to the most prominent sound you hear or pick a few different colors and see if you can find five things in your environment for each color.

Ironically, we attach our thoughts and feelings to situations because we think it gives us *control* over them. What really happens, though, is that we're allowing these situations to control *us*.

We allow our negative feelings about the jerk who cut us off in traffic to keep us feeling angry and hostile all day. He's gone! Your thoughts aren't affecting him at all! So, who's the one being negatively affected by all your angry thoughts? Only you!

Non-attachment isn't the same as being apathetic or avoidant. Going back to where I started, if action is necessary, put your focus there. But if not, let that cloud float on by!

HERE'S YOUR CHALLENGE FOR THE WEEK

Let's break free from some thought loops. Start by practicing being an observer of your thoughts. Remember, they come *from* you, but they only represent a *small part* of you, and that part is often stuck defending hurts from your past.

When you detect a repeating thought, decide if it's the seed for future action or just a cloud that got stuck.

If it's a seed, figure out the action. If it's a cloud, blow on it and let it pass on by.

Then, get back into the present. The present is usually pretty darn good. Or at least not terrible. Don't let the jerk from this morning's traffic take that away from you.

You've got this! See you next week.

NOTES

....

....

....

....

....

....

....

....

....

....

....

....

....

....

....

....

....

Find happiness where you least expect it

ONE SUMMER MORNING, I was chopping pineapple for my col-lege-aged son. He had mentioned that he enjoyed having yogurt and pineapple for breakfast at school, so I bought him some to have while he was home. The pre-chopped pineapple at our grocery store came in huge chunks, though, so it had gone uneaten.

Now, I knew he was perfectly capable of chopping his own fruit. Still, when I saw those huge chunks remaining in our refrigerator, I decided to do him a favor. He didn't *ask* me to do it, and I know he didn't *expect* me to either.

As I was chopping, I reflected on how, in the past, when I had *so many* family responsibilities on my plate, a task like this might have irritated me. I might have felt resentful about the amount of time

I spent serving others. I might have needed to step back and let others be more personally responsible for their needs.

But now, with both of my children in college, I was truly enjoying the opportunity to be of service. I felt happy as I chopped away.

Ironically, I was listening to a podcast about happiness.

Literally right after I noticed how happy I was in that moment, the presenter shared research about the disconnect between what we *think* will make us happy and what *actually* makes us happy. Data was gathered by pinging subjects randomly throughout the day and having them record what they were doing and how happy they felt.[1]

The results indicated that people reported their highest levels of happiness during ordinary moments. And there I was, chopping fruit and feeling happy!

Now, there's a catch. Ordinary moments can lead to happiness when we're *present* in the moment. If we're engaged in a mundane task but we're in a hurry—perhaps mentally complaining to ourselves (I call this "*mental bitching*") or wishing we were doing something else—happiness is low.

The big jolts of happiness we get from big activities, like a vacation, spa day, or buying a new car, diminish quickly. That's called **Hedonic Adaptation**. We return to our baseline level of happiness pretty rapidly.

And when we're not mindful of the joy we get from ordinary moments, we become blind to that joy (we do the same thing with *people*, taking our most important relationships for granted and losing sight of what these people add to our lives).

HERE'S YOUR CHALLENGE FOR THE WEEK

Let's maximize our chances of finding joy in ordinary moments!

What's a regular task you wouldn't typically describe as one that brings you *joy*? This week, make a conscious effort to be *present* while doing this task.

Start by reminding yourself that you *get* to do this task. There are far worse ways to spend time than folding laundry, doing yard work, sitting in meetings, or watching youth sports practices.

Pay attention to the little things you've "gone blind" to. Get present. Check in with your senses. Notice your surroundings as if for the first time. There are so many ways to inject gratitude and enjoyment into *any* activity!

Add music or use the time to practice observing your thoughts without attaching to them.

Try this with people, too. If you were meeting your friends and family for the first time, what would you notice about them? How would you describe them to others? What would draw you in and make you want to spend more time with them?

Then ask yourself—if *you* had been in the happiness study and were pinged during these ordinary moments, how happy would *you* report being?

With a little effort, the things we take for granted in our lives can continue to bring us happiness and joy. These simple things have the power to raise our happiness baseline. Without them, we become more desperate for short-term happiness boosts (Hedonic Adaptations) that don't last.

You've got this! See you next week.

NOTES

....

....

....

....

....

....

....

....

....

....

....

....

....

....

....

Sneak up on your deepest desires

I'M A MIDDLE-AGED woman whose children are in college, so it's not surprising that many of my friends are *also* middle-aged women with children in college.

As we approached the time when we would no longer have children at home, we were warned that this transition was often hard on couples. After years of the family centering around children, creating a new dynamic for connection can be difficult.

That's *not* what I've observed my friends (and clients) struggle with the most, though.

The most common struggle I've seen in my cohort has been deciding how to spend your extra time and energy once it's not consumed by parenting. This transition often includes decisions around career, purpose, and leisure time.

Identifying what you want in life can be much more difficult than it sounds, and this is true for *everyone*.

It can be tough to admit—to others *and* yourself—what you want. Your wants may feel unrealistic, overwhelming, or embarrassing. They might trigger a fear of rejection, failure, change, or disappointment.

Or, if you spent your whole life being told what you *should* want, you may have lost touch with what you *authentically* want.

And as is often true when we engage in behaviors that don't serve our best selves, we can be completely unaware that this is happening!

This **desire-blindness** is so common that I start every new coaching relationship with the same exercise. You can't pursue goals that will make your life more rewarding when you're not even sure what you want!

I have clients imagine that it's been a year since we finished working together, and they're reflecting on how incredibly happy they are. I give them a moment to fully marinate in the warmth and peace that comes with feeling content and fulfilled by your life.

Next, they decide that I'm someone who would appreciate hearing what they're up to, so they call me. They start the conversation with, "It's been an absolutely fantastic year. I'm so happy with the path I'm on right now. Over the past year, I've…"

And…*action!* I have my clients to take over from there. I instruct them to share whatever comes to mind without overthinking or editing themselves—to speak directly from that good feeling. I promise I won't judge them or hold them to anything they say. We'll use what comes up as one source of information to help guide future goals.

This exercise helps people *sneak up* on their deepest desires. If you take too much time to think, Anxious Mouse will try to talk you out of ideas that trigger his little mouse fears.

Downgrading your desires kills your soul. Let your soul speak! It's a good habit to get into. Action steps need to be small and realistic, but dreams don't.

HERE'S YOUR CHALLENGE FOR THE WEEK

Try this exercise for yourself. It's sometimes called "**future pacing**," a type of mental rehearsal. Imagining yourself achieving something helps the brain accept it as possible.

Pick a point in the future. It could be a few months or a few years from now. This is different from setting goals for the future, though. Remember, at this stage, you're not worried about choosing wants that are *realistic*. You're allowed to want what you want. Be honest with yourself first and figure out the details later.

The **what** and the **why** always come before the **how**.

Soak up the good feeling that comes with being happy with your life. Then, imagine the experiences that could be the source of this good feeling. Trick Anxious Mouse by imagining they've *already happened*. He has nothing to fear if you've already succeeded at getting what you want.

When you're done, write down everything you thought of. Tell yourself how much you love and appreciate yourself for vulnerably acknowledging these wants. This is such a special peek at your true self.

Some of these wants will be easy to translate into goals and actions. If you have some of those, pick one, plot a path, and give yourself a deadline for taking the first step.

For the big wants, live with them for a while. Just admitting them to yourself is a huge step. Over time, the *why* behind them might become apparent and lead to some manageable ideas.

Or you might need time to get comfortable with the idea of jumping in and going after something *big*. Either way, the most important outcome is that you're no longer silencing your true self.

You've got this! See you next week.

NOTES

....

....

....

....

....

....

....

....

....

....

....

....

....

....

....

....

....

WEEK 8

Build better boundaries

BOUNDARIES ARE ONE of my very favorite topics because, full disclosure, I wasn't skilled at setting them until my 40s! Based on the experiences of my friends and clients, I *know* I'm not alone.

When people think about "bad boundaries," they usually think about someone who can't say no and lets others trample all over them (guilty as charged!). While that's clearly a boundary issue, there are *four* kinds of **boundary difficulties**. I'll describe each in a minute, but first, let's clarify what boundaries are and why they're so important.

The purpose of a boundary is to define and protect our personal and emotional space. Healthy emotional boundaries foster self-respect and autonomy while supporting healthy relationships with others.

I use the analogy of **backpacks** and **book stacks** to help clients decide where their emotional and energetic boundaries should be.

This is a personal decision—a healthy boundary for you is what feels right for *you* and is flexible based on *your* circumstances.

There are elements of our lives that are ours to take care of. I call these our *backpack issues*. In normal circumstances, capable adults should be able to take care of the basics of their own life—a manageable load—like a backpack.

Sometimes, however, we have an extra load, more than we can fit in our backpack. I call these our *book stack issues*. Imagine someone walking out of a library carrying books piled up to their eyes. During challenging times or when we have more on our plates than we can manage, it's reasonable and wise to ask for help carrying these stacks of books.

If you imagine all situations as being divided into either backpack or book stack experiences, here are four types of boundary violations:

1. **Can't say no:** Most people think of this category when they think about establishing (or *not* establishing) boundaries. It's the person who gets overextended because they say yes to everything and everyone. They'll carry other people's backpacks and help with book stacks even if their muscles are about to give out. They probably truly want to be helpful, but they also don't want to disappoint.

2. **Can't hear no:** This person expects help with both their book stack *and* their backpack, regardless of what others are already carrying. They're usually persistent and feel entitled.

Their assertiveness is sometimes viewed as a positive trait, but in reality, it's often linked to their inability to manage their own lives, a sign of emotional immaturity.

3. **Can't hear yes:** This person doesn't ask for help or accept it when it's offered. They've always 'got it' on their own. They wouldn't *think* of expecting someone else to carry their backpack, and they'll get crushed under their own book stack before seeking (or accepting) assistance. This can look like personal strength, but it really stems from discomfort with vulnerability.

4. **Can't say yes:** This person doesn't notice when others need help. They take care of their own backpack and don't believe that others' book stacks are any of their concern. Their boundary issue keeps them closed off to others and comes from a place of self-focus and a belief in the importance of personal accountability.

HERE'S YOUR CHALLENGE FOR THE WEEK

When you read those four descriptions, did one resonate with you? Are you aware of how unhealthy boundaries impact your life? Do you tend to have no boundaries, flexible boundaries, or rigid boundaries? How do your boundaries differ in different situations?

Play with these four types of boundary struggles this week. Notice when you experience them and when you see them in others.

As is always true, understanding the *why* behind your unhealthy boundaries will help you shift them. What beliefs lead you to be too rigid or flexible with your boundaries? What do you think might happen if you shift your boundaries? Do you worry that people will reject you? Judge you? Take advantage of you? View you as weak?

In the same way that you question Anxious Mouse, question your boundary beliefs. Ask yourself *what else* could be true, and then make choices that support backpacks as personal responsibilities and book stacks as opportunities to give or receive support.

It's *your responsibility* to care for yourself. Healthy boundaries protect your energy and your peace, and everyone deserves to set them in a way that feels empowering.

And while it might upset people, it's a gift to nudge them to care for their own backpacks. Accepting unhealthy boundaries from others enables them to remain emotionally immature. You prevent others from growing into *their* authentic selves when you over-care for them.

Whether or not people recognize it, your healthy boundaries create win-win opportunities. They help us all balance our self-care responsibilities with our contribution to community. By honoring your boundaries, you empower yourself and others to thrive in harmony.

You've got this! See you next week.

NOTES

....
....
....
....
....
....
....
....
....
....
....
....
....
....
....

Two more ways to increase your happiness

A FEW WEEKS ago, I challenged you to practice being present during ordinary moments because studies show that's where happiness hides. Today, I'll give you two more easy sources of happiness.

First, research shows that time spent outside increases happiness. This was another finding from the study where people were pinged throughout the day and asked to report their level of happiness and what they were doing at that moment.

Even when other factors were controlled for, people reported feeling happier when they were outside—and this had nothing to do with the weather. People reported just as much additional happiness when the weather was cold, rainy, or cloudy as when it was warm and sunny. Yeah, sure, it might be more *comfortable* or *convenient* to go outside on lovely days, but from a happiness standpoint, it's all the same.

Second, people are happier when they're away from their phones. Researchers tested a variety of conditions with phones present and with phones out of reach. No matter what the subjects were doing, they consistently reported greater happiness when positioning their phones out of reach.[2]

Turning the phone upside down didn't have the same effect, nor did turning it off and leaving it within reach. It turns out that just being near our phones distracts us and increases our level of anxiety. If we see it, we must check it!

I'm sure neither one of these findings is mind-boggling to you. We were built to be in nature and present with our surroundings. Being indoors for too long makes us feel stir-crazy. We enjoy activities that put us in nature, such as gardening, hiking, skiing, swimming—even just laying on a blanket on the beach or at the park.

And, as valuable as our smartphones can be, most of us have had moments where we fantasized about throwing them into the ocean and freeing ourselves from this electronic tether. Deep down, we know our constant digital connection is costing us peace and happiness.

HERE'S YOUR CHALLENGE FOR THE WEEK

This is an easy one—get outside! And put your phone out of reach now and then!

Where are you *right now* on these two dimensions? This week, challenge yourself to take it up a notch. Aim to increase your outdoor time by 10 minutes at least three days this week. You get bonus points if those extra 10 minutes are in inclement weather.

Lunchtime is a great time to get outdoors. A quick outdoor walk is a great way to boost your energy, mood, and brain power for the afternoon.

Try taking an extra step to increase time away from your phone as well. Do you have a "phone basket" somewhere in your house? If not, get one! Or just use a bowl or a drawer.

Mealtimes are a great place to start. Put the phone out of sight in its designated resting place during meals, even if you're eating alone. If you already do that, think of another time you'd like to be more present and make that a no-phone time, too.

It's so nice to know that moments of happiness are easy to achieve. You don't need a mountain of money—just intention, action, and presence. Try these two challenges and notice how much you raise your happiness baseline by next week.

You've got this! See you next week.

NOTES

....

....

....

....

....

....

....

....

....

....

....

....

....

....

....

Make every day a day worth celebrating

EVERY COACHING SESSION I hold starts by celebrating the good things my clients have experienced since our last session.

Sometimes, this celebration could last the entire hour. Other times, my clients need to dig *really* deep to think of anything they consider worth celebrating.

No matter how rough things are, they always eventually find *something* for us to celebrate. (Partly because they know they have no choice!) It's during those rough times that celebrating the good is most important. Tough times can blind us to the good we're still experiencing.

Celebrating the good in our lives trains our brains to *notice* the good in our lives. And, as you'll see in this week's challenge, with a little proactive effort, you can ensure every day has moments of joy and experiences to celebrate.

HERE'S YOUR CHALLENGE FOR THE WEEK

Every morning for the next week, before you even get out of bed, ask yourself what could go well for you that day. What might bring you joy, move you closer to a goal, or feel like a win? What could be something you'd celebrate at the end of the day? (Or in a coaching session with me?)

There are two advantages to doing this first thing in the morning:

1. First, if you can't think of anything positive coming up that day, you can proactively brainstorm something to *add* to your day.

2. Second, when experiencing something celebration-worthy, you'll be primed to *notice* the win so you can soak it up in the moment.

It's also a great idea to reflect on the good things we already have in our lives. Studies show that gratitude is associated with the following:

- increased happiness and well-being,

- decreased stress and anxiety,

- greater satisfaction with relationships,

- improved sleep,

- higher self-esteem, and

- higher resilience in tough times.[3]

And remember, celebrations aren't just for big wins. Some days, just being alive, having food to eat, or having supportive people in our lives is the best we can come up with. It's during these low times that identifying the good is most important. It can reset our mindset and attitude so we can access the benefits of gratitude.

With a little effort in the morning, we can increase the chance of good things happening every day and ensure we'll pause and enjoy them when they do. That's definitely time well spent!

You've got this! See you next week.

NOTES

Decipher your relationship habits

WHETHER THEY ADMIT it or not, every human craves deep, meaningful, connected relationships—but sometimes, those can seem as mythical as unicorns.

There are many factors that influence how successful we are at connecting with others. **Attachment style** is a big one.

Your attachment style is largely influenced by the relationships you had with your early caregivers. This is where you learned what safety feels like, which determines how you'll set boundaries, communicate needs, and give and receive love in future relationships.

Understanding your attachment style can help you see why you sometimes sabotage your connection to others and why others sometimes do the same to you.

Before you get your weekly challenge, I'll briefly describe the three main attachment styles (and one particularly troublesome hybrid).

Secure Attachment: You have a positive view of yourself and others, feel seen and valued, and enjoy being in close, intimate relationships. You feel comfortable communicating your needs and feelings to others and are skilled at reading and responding to others' emotional cues.

Anxious Attachment: You feel most at ease when you're in close connection with others. However, you often fear that others don't feel as strongly about you as you feel about them, leaving you feeling rejected. This can lead to anxiety, low self-esteem, and clingy, insecure behaviors.

Avoidant Attachment: You repress your feelings and needs and wear your independence and self-reliance as a badge of honor. You may feel suffocated when relationships get too close. You push others away when relationships deepen and believe that negative qualities in others are the source of your need for space.

Disorganized: A small percentage of people deeply crave connection but also feel triggered by it. This leads to a pattern of seeking closeness and then pulling away, which can be confusing and challenging for others to navigate.

First, spend some time thinking about *your* attachment style. Did one of these styles resonate with you right away? Be an observer of yourself this week, a scientist studying *you*.

Keep in mind that these categories aren't all-or-none. We usually exhibit elements of different styles in different situations and relationships. For example, you might feel secure with friends but anxious in romantic relationships. Or maybe you had secure relationships at your last job, but the climate at your new company fosters competitive, anxious connections.

If you need help identifying your attachment style or want to learn more, search "attachment style quiz" online. There are quite a few free ones.

Once you have a sense of how you show up in relationships, ask yourself *why*. What positive and/or difficult experiences have you had with attachment? Who in your life has loved and accepted you as you are? Who has been inconsistent, demeaning, or rigid in their expectations of you? Have you known people who modeled how to manage emotions and communicate authentically? Not everyone is exposed to these skills growing up.

Finally, come up with some statements you can tell yourself—and others—that will communicate how you're feeling so your actions aren't misinterpreted.

Here are some examples:

- When you're feeling anxiously attached, share that some-times you need reassurance that the relationship is important because your mind tends to search for signs of abandonment.

- When you're feeling avoidant, share that sometimes close-ness overwhelms you, and taking a moment for some space doesn't indicate how you feel about the relationship.

Share the good stuff, too! When you feel securely attached, express how much you enjoy being in the other person's company and how much you value the relationship.

If you're lucky enough to easily feel a secure connection to others (about 50% of the population is[4]), remember that this doesn't come naturally to everyone. With self-awareness and good communi-cation, though, attachment styles don't have to have toxic effects on relationships.

You've got this! See you next week.

NOTES

....

....

....

....

....

....

....

....

....

....

....

....

....

....

....

....

Reconnect with your best self

LIFE IS COMPLICATED, and we all wear many hats throughout our lives. Each of those hats carries a different set of expectations and changes us a bit. Over time, it's easy to lose ourselves and the connection to our inner voice and our truth.

But our essence, our true self, never changes.

As the version of ourselves that we present to the world and our 'true selves' get further apart, we become unsettled. We often label this feeling as anxiety and blame the people and events in our lives for our discontent. We have no conscious awareness that the source is actually *inside* of us—our disconnection from self.

There's a way to reconnect with your essence, though. Having an anchor you can go to when you're feeling scattered, lost, or powerless can bring you back to yourself. It can help you regain control and own your value and purpose in life.

This week's challenge can help you realign with your true self when you're feeling unsettled and help you emerge from a place of fear, doubt, and insecurity into a place of calm confidence.

HERE'S YOUR CHALLENGE FOR THE WEEK

We're going to do an art project! Please do this activity when you have at least half an hour of free time.

First, get a piece of paper and something to write with. A pencil is fine, but you can certainly go all-in with colored pencils or markers and make this a full-on art project.

Next, sit where you can have a quiet moment to yourself. Get settled in your seat and think about a time when you felt really good about yourself. Maybe you were experiencing a success, overcoming a challenge, participating in an activity you love, or having a wonderful moment of connection.

Let that good feeling wash all over you. Note *where* in your body you feel it. As we discussed a few weeks ago, we hold our feelings in our bodies. Take some time if this isn't easily identifiable. It's in there somewhere!

Then, imagine this good feeling as an image. When I first did this exercise, I felt a warm glow in my chest and imagined it as the sun. Your good feeling can be represented in any way that feels right to you. I've had people say it was a puppy, a heart, a high-five, a racecar, a volleyball, a rainbow, or a sunset. I even had a teenage girl identify it as a box of bright eyeshadows!

Draw this happiness image on your paper. If it feels right, name your "best self feeling" too. I've heard Champ, Sunny, Spike, Mom, and Love Muffin. Anything that will help you bring this image to mind later.

As you hold this image in your mind, say to yourself, "I am…" What qualities are you exhibiting when you feel lit up like this? Write these words all around your drawing.

Consider how you show up in different areas of your life and how people who know you well would describe you.

Here's the key to this exercise—*keep doing this for at least five minutes!* The first few words will come easily and will probably be the standard go-to words you use to describe your strengths. With time, though, you'll be amazed at how many other positive qualities pop into your mind.

Don't edit yourself! There's nothing too silly or insignificant.

My first few words were smart, compassionate, good listener, and even-keeled. When I dug deeper, qualities such as brave, flexible, resilient, peaceful, present, aware, rational, inquisitive, and open-minded bubbled up. They're not the main ways I identify myself, but they definitely resonate with me.

If you're being honest with yourself, when you look back at your list, you'll find yourself thinking, *"Dang*—yes, I really *AM* all of these things!"* I've seen it happen countless times with clients. Our weaknesses come to mind easily, but we all have *so many* exceptional qualities we take for granted.

With any activity like this, where you're trying to get beyond your conscious mind, you must give it time. Your conscious mind is a gatekeeper that wants to keep you from getting too vulnerable or authentic. If you stick with the task, your conscious mind will eventually loosen its grip, and your connection to your true self will bubble to the surface.

When you're done, put your best self-artwork where you'll see it daily. My sunshine is taped to the pencil mug on my desk.

I know firsthand that this works! In moments when I feel imposter syndrome creeping in, I look at my sun and read my "I am" words, and the reconnection with my best self-qualities gives me the confidence to move forward.

You've got this! See you next week.

NOTES

....

....

....

....

....

....

....

....

....

....

....

....

....

....

....

....

Adopt positive mindsets

ONE OF THE best things about being a coach is that I have a wealth of strategies to draw on when *I'm* in need of a mental boost.

Years ago, after watching my son's baseball team struggle through a playoff game, I had one of those moments. On the whole, it had been a tough weekend. There were some exciting moments, but the team never gained any momentum. To add insult to injury, it started pouring right after the final game.

Baseball (and life) is like that sometimes. Some days just aren't going to be your day.

Later, back at my hotel and in dry clothes, I looked out the window at the gray sky. I needed a boost. I was over feeling sad.

I dug into my mental file of positive mindsets, and a few life truths came up that felt relevant for the weekend. These five stood out as particularly powerful—not just to pull you up from a rough day, but to empower your attitude *every* day:

1. **Be here now**. Sometimes, 'here and now' is sad (like it was right after the game), but imagining future sadness or reliving past sadness prolongs your pain unnecessarily. Get out of your head and into the moment. There's usually a lot of good in the present.

2. **Whatever you feel now won't be how you feel forever**. Take some deep breaths and let the tough feelings pass through you. This goes for the tough times *and* the good times, though, so make a conscious effort to soak up the good when you can.

3. **You have survived 100% of your challenges so far**. When you're experiencing a challenge, reflect on the strengths and skills you've called on in the past to pull yourself through your tough times. Call on them again and persevere!

4. **You are whole and worthy as you are *right now*!** Strive for consistent growth *not* because who you are right now is deficient, but because all living things are meant to grow. It's your purpose, and it makes life interesting and enjoyable.

5. **No matter what paths you didn't take in the past, everything is still possible**. (Well, not *everything*, but the essence of everything.) You weren't ready for any path you

didn't take in the past. There have been no mistakes. Figure out what you want right now, and take the first step today.

HERE'S YOUR CHALLENGE FOR THE WEEK

Which one of these five mindsets resonates most with you right now? Write it down (with your hand—don't type it) and put it where you'll see it every day.

I went through a long period where I had difficulty controlling spiraling thoughts. I repeated, "Be here now" to myself regularly throughout the day, and it did wonders to ground me in the present. Depending on the situation, I've called on each of these mindsets throughout my life when I needed a boost to show up strong.

At the end of the week, reflect on how your chosen mindset served you. Without it, how might you have allowed yourself to stay small, fearful, distracted, stuck, or lost?

There are lots of things we can't control in life, and those things get Anxious Mouse squeaking. Your thoughts and your mindset are things you *can* control, though. Proving to yourself that you have power and choice in your life builds self-esteem and self-confidence. Those are some good reasons to work at becoming a diligent master of your mind and your mindsets!

You've got this! See you next week.

NOTES

Use your pain to increase your peace

HAVE YOU EVER experienced an intense emotional reaction seemingly out of nowhere? These moments, often referred to as "**triggers**," are like setting off emotional landmines that were buried deep within us.

Any type of stimuli can serve as a trigger. Everyday situations, words, actions, sights, sounds, smells, feelings, and even people can unexpectedly stir up a strong emotional response.

We often feel the reaction in our body before we have any idea of what's happening. It can show up as a stomachache, anxious energy, or muscle tension. We often associate these feelings with negative emotions such as anxiety, fear, anger, sadness, and shame.

Unfortunately, we usually mistakenly assume that these reactions are related to our *current* circumstances. Learning to identify when we're experiencing a trigger and where the trigger originated can help us respond to *reality* instead of dragging our emotional past into the present.

I once had a client who believed her partner was no longer physically attracted to her. Anytime he said anything she interpreted as being about her weight or her appearance, she'd explode. Her real wound, however, had nothing to do with him.

She came from a big family and felt insecure about being loved by her parents as a child. Not feeling secure in close relationships was an old wound. When it got activated, such as feeling rejected because of her appearance, she looked for causes in her immediate environment.

To paraphrase one of my favorite quotes, *"she bled on her husband even though he wasn't the one who cut her."*

She could have been a supermodel or had a partner who endlessly professed his love, and her root issue would remain. She would never feel safe in a partner's love until she addressed her old feeling of being unsure about her parents' love.

HERE'S YOUR CHALLENGE FOR THE WEEK

Be on the lookout for situations and experiences that create intense emotional reactions in you. Remember, you might be labeling your feeling as anger or anxiety, or cry even though you don't feel sad.

Step back and look at the big picture. What specific part of the situation is rubbing you the wrong way? Does it remind you of something from your past? If so, what emotion did that old situation create in you?

Note: If your trigger creates significant distress or feels related to a serious situation, such as abuse, please seek the assistance of a licensed therapist. You deserve to live in peace without reliving the stress and pain your triggers call forward from your past.

Now, let's tease apart the past from the present. Take off your "trigger glasses," the ones that see the present through the lens of your past, and challenge your interpretation of what's happening *now*.

Make a list of *factual* statements about what you're experiencing that don't require making assumptions, guessing at intentions, or reading other people's minds.

The brain has difficulty discerning between the past, the present, and the (imagined) future. Consciously anchoring in the present helps you see the difference.

Finally, let's use the trigger to learn about yourself. Do you have an idea of when you first started experiencing this trigger? Are there patterns or commonalities in the things that trigger you? A person, place, experience, or event? Sensory experiences are common triggers because senses are powerfully connected to your memories.

Could the trigger be connected to a core belief of yours? Can you challenge that belief? Could other things be true? How does this belief serve you? What possibilities might arise if you shift your belief?

Emotional growth comes from accepting your triggers as opportunities for healing rather than sources of anger and pain. You can't let go of what you don't go through. Thanking your triggers for exposing past hurts opens you to a more emotionally healthy future.

You've got this! See you next week.

NOTES

....

....

....

....

....

....

....

....

....

....

....

....

....

....

....

....

WEEK 15

Gift yourself some self-compassion

SINCE YOU WERE interested in this book, I bet I can guess a few things about you. For one, I bet you're pretty nice to other people. People who aren't kind to others are rarely interested in self-improvement and coaching. They're convinced that all their problems come from *outside* of themselves. They think everyone *else* needs to change.

On the other hand, people who are interested in personal growth are often very hard on themselves. They acknowledge that they have room to grow and are sensitive to where they believe they fall short.

Self-critical people often struggle with perfectionism and procrastination. This type of thinking is also related to anxiety, depression, poor resilience, low self-confidence, impaired decision-making, and unsatisfying relationships.[5]

The harmful effects of self-criticism also go beyond the mind. Being hard on yourself has physical consequences. Psychological tension can affect heart health, muscle tension, immune response, and inflammation.

Self-critical people tend to fall into the trap of believing that being hard on themselves is the key to self-improvement. How can you improve if you don't hold yourself to a high standard? If you don't put a spotlight on your weaknesses and deficits?

The answer is **self-compassion**. Self-compassion isn't a weakness; it's actually fertilizer for growth.

Self-compassion allows you to accept yourself as whole and worthy as you are right now. It *also* acknowledges that if you open yourself to more, you'll continue to grow from where you are today.

Self-compassion is expansive, whereas self-criticism is restrictive. You can only have self-respect with self-compassion. And if *you* don't respect yourself, you shouldn't expect anyone else to either.

HERE'S YOUR CHALLENGE FOR THE WEEK

Here are five steps to try this week to shift your self-treatment from *negative* to *nurturing*:

1. As always, the first step is becoming aware of your internal conversations. They'll go off in all kinds of unproductive

directions if you don't keep an eye on them! Start noticing the types of conversations you have with yourself.

2. Challenge any critical self-talk you discover. Ask yourself if it's accurate, based in truth, and supportive of your growth.

3. Substitute compassionate language for criticism and self-hate. What would you say to a friend in this situation? How would you support and encourage them?

4. Get realistic. You will not be perfect—no one is! Embrace the idea that imperfection is part of being human and mistakes are part of learning and growth. When you make a mistake, tell yourself your humanity is showing. Make it funny and keep things light!

5. Identify one action, no matter how small or easy, that you could take to show up differently in the future. This is how you create personal growth, one small step at a time.

Remember, this doesn't mean you *will* show up differently, but at least make the *attempt*. Then, you can fine-tune your plan as needed.

If you're at war with yourself, you can never win. Self-criticism is a constant attack on the self, and you deserve better. We all do!

If someone else did this to you, you could set boundaries and limit your time with them. But you can't get away from yourself, so give yourself the chance to *thrive* by supporting, encouraging, and loving yourself.

You've got this! See you next week.

NOTES

....

....

....

....

....

....

....

....

....

....

....

....

....

....

....

Magically get your needs met

BEING CALLED "NEEDY" is usually meant to be an insult. Needy people are thought of as weak, incompetent, emotionally fragile, and unable to take care of themselves.

But we all need things, and sometimes we need *other people* to help us meet those needs.

The way we shy away from expressing our needs is often tied to gender. Women may feel like they shouldn't *burden* others or come across as too *demanding*. This leads to indirect requests and passive-aggressive reactions, neither of which are good for relationships (or getting what you need).

This could sound like:

- "Why doesn't anyone ever put their dishes in the dishwasher?"

- "Am I the only one who knows where the dishwasher is?"

- "I'd like to just get up and walk away after dinner, too."

I'm a woman, so I get it. I understand what these sentences really mean. ("PUT YOUR DAMN DISHES IN THE DISHWASHER!") And I get that there's some frustration under that meaning.

Men, on the other hand, often struggle to express *emotional* needs. Society has led them to believe they're only allowed to *need* things that don't require vulnerability. They can be direct at work or about impersonal things—they can need pizza or a new set of golf clubs—but stereotypical views of masculinity don't allow for needing emotional support or human connection.

If you can't communicate your needs directly, then you're expecting others to be mind readers. News flash—mind readers don't exist! You're just setting yourself up for a lifetime of disappointment.

When my clients use soft, indirect, wishy-washy language to discuss something I can tell is important to them, I call them out and ask if they can try using the magic word.

You just read it at least ten times—the magic word is "*need*."

If you could state what you need and label it as such without all the emotional baggage around not wanting to appear weak or not feeling worthy, you'd have a much better chance of *getting* what you desire.

This could sound like, "I need help cleaning up after dinner. Please put your dishes in the dishwasher when you're done eating," or "I need a hug and to share something I've been struggling with."

That's it! Done! So simple!

You don't need to overexplain, get defensive, yell, cry, pout, or attack.

You're allowed to need things! Tell people what you need so you can have a chance of getting it.

Needing doesn't make you self-centered or soft. It's part of your tenderness as a human. You give others the ability to honor your needs when you share them authentically. This is connection and self-care at its finest!

HERE'S YOUR CHALLENGE FOR THE WEEK

Share your needs! If you need a pep talk to do this, that's okay. Tell yourself, "Linda says it's *okay* to have needs."

Catch yourself before you get all wishy-washy and minimize your worthiness, or before you choke down your vulnerable desire for comfort and connection.

Repeat after me, "I need…"

Say it often, and practice until it feels comfortable. Express anything important with an "I" statement, and label it as a need if that's your truth.

Expressing your need isn't a demand; it's a calm statement of truth. It clearly communicates to others how they can serve you.

If being this direct feels emotional and stirs up a physical reaction in your body, pause and do a few rounds of slow breathing. Practice making "statements of need" to yourself once you feel a sense of calm in your body.

This might initially feel excessive, but you'll get used to it. You're not being demanding, and you're not being weak. You're being clear and giving people the chance to make a difference in your life.

When people communicate clearly with each other, so much unnecessary conflict can be avoided. And the bonus is you'll finally allow yourself to get what you really need.

You've got this! See you next week.

NOTES

....
....
....
....
....
....
....
....
....
....
....
....
....
....
....
....
....
....

WEEK 17

A cure for FOHN (Fear of Hearing No)

HOW DO YOU react when you hear the word "no?"

Even if you're able to persevere in the face of rejection, "no" still makes most people uncomfortable. It feels like rejection, and we're built to desire the safe acceptance of others.

But *fearing* "no" can hold us back, so let's look at this another way: What would you ask for in life if you *knew* the answer would be "*yes?*"

With a simple mindset shift, we can help our brains relax when they encounter a "no"—and that can help us transform that "no" into a "yes."

The trick is to think of every "no" as an invitation into connection rather than a personal rejection.

Whoever said "no" to you *also* has a brain that's focused on safety and survival.

"No" often really means, "I wasn't expecting that. That's scary." It's often a defensive reaction.

Brains like consistency. You're alive right now, so your brain gets comfort from maintaining the status quo. Red flags go up for anything new, different, or outside your comfort zone.

I've had many clients who were fed up with their spouses because their spouses said "no" to *everything*. These clients complained that their spouses were negative, boring, unadventurous, or controlling. Or they took these "no's" personally and decided their spouse was against anything *they* wanted. That's incredibly toxic to a relationship!

I guided these clients to manage their relationships with two mindset shifts. First, how lucky they were that their spouse was predictable! When there's a pattern, we can find its root.

And second, if they could see this "no" as a first step rather than a rejection, they could get it to soften.

To soften a "no" into a "yes," investigate the fear that's behind it. Instead of getting defensive or shutting down, give the other person space to adjust to a new idea.

What does this look like? Curiosity is always an excellent first step, so ask some questions. Questions help you gather information and show the other person that you care about their perspective.

Here are some simple phrases to try:

- "I'd love to hear what you're thinking."

- "I'm curious—what about that doesn't sit well with you?"

- "That was a really quick response. Could you share more?"

- "What information can I provide to help you feel more comfortable with this idea?"

How do *you* feel when reading these questions? To me, they feel like a door opening rather than a wall going up. They're invitations for collaboration rather than conversational dead-ends.

Even if you don't get from "no" to "yes," your questions will help you better understand the other person. Your questions also tell them something about *you*. They show you're someone they can trust to care about their perspective.

That's what we all want more than anything else—*to know that we matter!*

HERE'S YOUR CHALLENGE FOR THE WEEK

To shift the way you react to the word "no," you need to *hear* the word "no." This week, ask someone for something you think they'll reject. Push the boundaries. Your goal is to hear "no," so go big here. Face your FOHN.

Then, instead of freezing and feeling rejected, imagine that their "no" was really their way of reaching out to connect with you. What could you ask them? What do they want you to know about them? Why did your request activate their Anxious Mouse?

Mindfully keep your focus on connection rather than outcome. Be an explorer and see where this takes you. The answer might remain "no," but this process softens the sharp edges.

Your curiosity and connection will help people drop their armor and expand their comfort zones. Just be careful what you ask for—you're going to get more "yeses" than you're used to!

You've got this! See you next week.

NOTES

....

....

....

....

....

....

....

....

....

....

....

....

....

....

....

WEEK 18

Rein in your racing brain

NO MATTER HOW good you are at setting boundaries and managing time, it's easy to slip into mental overwhelm.

It can happen when you have an abundance of blessings in your life, like a busy family or a successful career. It can also happen in tough times, such as managing health issues or major life changes.

I spiraled into a state of overwhelm when a crisis required me to reschedule a complicated series of travel plans. My brain raced as I struggled to determine all the reservations that needed to be changed. Like dominoes, everything needed to be rebooked in the correct sequence to ensure the new plans still fit together correctly.

As my mind jumped wildly (and ineffectively) among all the pieces that had been impacted, I remembered an activity I give my clients when they struggle with similar situations:

- The *brain dump*!

In a brain dump, you take all the thoughts swimming around in your brain and write them down on paper. This is not the same as a to-do list. A to-do list helps you *remember* all the things you need to do, while a brain dump allows the piece of paper to be a *container* for your thoughts.

You can't focus when your mind is bouncing from thought to thought. This is the same way our brains operate when we're trying to multi-task, and it's a very inefficient way of thinking.

Once you've "downloaded" everything on your mind, choose the *one thing* you'll focus on first. Then, place the paper out of sight.

Now you can direct your full attention to this single thing—which is how humans work best—secure in the knowledge that when you're ready, the rest of your thoughts have been saved.

I tried this with my travel plans, and it worked like a charm. My brain dump not only helped me focus my thoughts but also allowed me to relax. I no longer had that anxious feeling that I was forgetting something. All my thoughts were safely held on my brain dump list. I'd get to the next domino when I was ready.

Seeing my thoughts on paper also created a big picture vision of my task. It's hard to see the whole puzzle when you're holding all the individual pieces in your memory.

Taking ten minutes for a brain dump allowed me to be more efficient and get out of fight-or-flight mode. That was definitely ten minutes well spent!

HERE'S YOUR CHALLENGE FOR THE WEEK

Try a brain dump! Even if you're only trying to hold a few things in your mind, see how it feels to transfer them to paper.

Then, look at the list with your calm mind. If something needs to be done *now*, put a checkmark next to that item. Then, put the list away.

Return to the list when you're ready to identify the next task to focus on. Give each item a time limit if you're under a time crunch.

Every time Anxious Mouse pops up and starts to worry about "all the things," let him know you have everything accounted for and send him off to his burrow.

Brain dumps can help quiet your mind before sleep, as well. Unfortunately, your brain often kicks into overdrive once you're cozy and relaxed in bed. Slowing down at bedtime gives your mind the space to remember all the things you couldn't attend to during the day.

Keep a brain dump pad by your bedside to download these thoughts as they come up. A calm mind is much more conducive to sleep than one racing with thoughts for tomorrow.

You've got this! See you next week.

NOTES

....

....

....

....

....

....

....

....

....

....

....

....

....

....

....

....

Manage the anxious energy in your life

I'M GOING TO do a little flip-flop on you this week. The intention of this book is to help you change your life by making shifts within *yourself*.

We only truly have the power to change ourselves. No matter how hard we try through inspiration, persuasion, or manipulation, we can't force change on other people.

But let's be honest. Sometimes, other people's anxiety challenges our peace and happiness. We can sense that they're having a rough time and wish we could do something to help them.

One of my good friends has a very anxious husband. His constant worrying drives her crazy, drains her energy, and limits their time together. He won't travel with her or do anything adventurous because he focuses on the potential problems with everything she suggests.

You can't *make* people like this change, but you *can* offer them support in a productive way. When the people around us feel less anxious, everyone in their circle benefits from their relaxed energy.

Before we get to your challenge, let's do a little anxiety review. Anxiety is produced when someone worries about *potential future threats*. Anxiety can cause people to avoid situations, react in anger, become defensive, and behave in ways that seem irrational.

If someone was reacting to an *actual* problem in the *present*, we could help them. It's hard to help with anxiety, though, since the reaction isn't in response to what's going on right now.

You can't be your best self in the present when your body is preparing to protect you from a perceived future attack on your safety.

Dealing with anxious people usually doesn't bring out our best, either. We often react to other people's anxious energy by becoming tense, irritated, dismissive, frustrated, defensive, or hostile. Sometimes we even take on other people's anxiety as our own.

Now you've got *two* people charged up about a possible future event. Someone's got to ground this interaction in the present!

Try these five steps the next time you notice someone avoiding, defending, shaming, blaming, acting irrationally, or over-relying on your support. They're designed to gently encourage people to discover where they might be experiencing anxiety and help them challenge the reality of their worries.

(You can use these steps on *yourself* as well when you notice *your* anxious energy oozing out onto others.)

1. Instead of pointing out what you're noticing in a way that could feel like an attack, such as "You're being a real jerk!" try curiously commenting on what you're observing. For example, "Whenever I suggest we try a new restaurant, I notice you try to talk me out of it."

2. Validate the reaction: "I get it; there's a lot of comfort in going to places that are familiar."

3. Ask questions to help the anxious person reflect on the source of their reaction: "When I suggest something new, do you have a sense of what runs through your mind? Do you remember having a bad experience with something new?"

4. Ask what would make this situation easier for them to manage: "If you went to a new restaurant and enjoyed yourself, what might that look like?"

5. Offer suggestions to help them gently lean into their worries so they can test if they're based in truth: "Would you be willing to try someplace new if we did some research first so you could get familiar with it? What about if *you* picked a new place to try?

One caveat here is that you are *never* to accept being treated abusively so someone else can avoid facing their anxiety. In those cases, start with these three steps:

1. State how this treatment makes you feel: "I feel devalued when you criticize me for wanting to try new things."

2. Set a clear boundary: "I won't participate in these conversations if we can't speak to each other kindly and respectfully. I want to find an option we can both be excited about, but shaming and teasing aren't helpful."

3. Set a consequence: "From now on, when you start criticizing me, the conversation is over, and I'm going to leave the room."

What we all want more than anything is to be seen and accepted for who we are. You can help anxious people by showing them that you're empathetic to their experience and open to helping them uncover the source of their discomfort. But—you can't *make* people play along! Offer them this gift, but also protect yourself.

If you put in the effort, sometimes you'll end up with the best-case scenario—a more pleasant person to deal with *and* a friend or loved one with less anxiety.

You've got this! See you next week.

NOTES

....

....

....

....

....

....

....

....

....

....

....

....

....

....

....

WEEK 20

Ground yourself in the present

I STARTED PRACTICING yoga in the summer of 2022. I was looking for more variety in my physical training and thought yoga would add a nice balance to running and weight workouts.

It turned out that yoga's *combination* of the physical with the mental and spiritual (which is not the same as religious) was what hooked me. In hindsight, it's really the perfect combination of my interests.

We've talked about this before, but it's hard to manage our racing minds. The guides at my studio start each class with the invitation to stay present and enjoy the gift of an hour devoted to our well-being.

One of these guides *continuously* repeats the reminder to stay present. This might seem excessive to some, but I really appreciate the frequent prompts. For me, keeping my mind "between the four corners of the mat," as they say in yoga, is a much bigger struggle than the physical poses.

During one of her classes, she worded the reminder a little differently. She said, "*Stay present in your gratitude.*" The phrase struck me like a lightning bolt right in my chest.

When the topic of tattoos comes up in conversation, I always tell people that if I ever get one, I'll have "Be here now" tattooed on the inside of my wrist. That's how important—and powerful—I think this centering practice is.

But to find *gratitude* in your present felt even *more* powerful!

Being in the present moment is beneficial, but it does take effort. Since our minds never shut off, it's impossible to just *be*. To keep your mind in the present, you need a place for your thoughts to land so they don't wander into the past and future.

Focusing on your breath is a common practice to help you ground yourself in the present. It's always with you, and it's happening in the moment.

Another way to harness your thoughts in the present is to focus on your senses. We've talked about this before, too. Noticing what you're hearing or seeing from moment to moment focuses your thoughts on your surroundings.

Those are both lovely practices. One connects you with your physical body and life force, and the other connects you with your environment. But connecting with *gratitude* for what you're experiencing *at that moment* takes the power of this practice to another level.

Connecting with gratitude in the present wrangles your thoughts into the here and now and forces you to become consciously aware of the good you're experiencing *right now*.

No matter how crappy your day has been, you can *always* find something to be grateful for in the moment. I'm positive about this! I've seen it in those clients who swear they have nothing to celebrate and then come up with a laundry list of good things once they widen their view beyond their story of woe.

HERE'S YOUR CHALLENGE FOR THE WEEK

Our minds wander constantly; this is just how they're built. But our fears, anxieties, hurts, traumas, doubts, resentments, regrets, etc., live in this wandering. Sadly, we rarely mind-wander about happy things unless we intentionally focus on positive memories or anticipations.

The good news is that this means you can always benefit from finding gratitude in the moment!

To make sure it happens, set a goal, such as three times per day. Anchor the practice to other events in your day, such as getting in your car, eating, or brushing your teeth. Put sticky note reminders in your environment so you don't forget while you're building this new habit.

When it's time for a gratitude moment, pull yourself into the present by asking yourself what you're grateful for *at that moment*—not yesterday or earlier in the day, and not in the future—*right then!*

With practice, the instinct to identify gratitude will pop into your mind whenever your mind wanders into negative territory.

When you're dreading an upcoming meeting, mentally complaining about the driver in front of you, or wishing you had handled a situation differently—bam! Switch to, "What am I grateful for *right now?*"

And just like that, you'll ground yourself in the present *and* shift into a more positive, productive mindset—two powerful practices wrapped up in one!

You've got this! See you next week.

NOTES

Hack your fear of failure

WOULDN'T IT BE nice if our brain's primary function was to help us achieve happiness or success? Or maybe to produce rational thought, free from emotional influence, or to connect with other people, or to conjure creative brilliance?

In reality, our brain's top concern is more basic than that—it's to keep us alive.

That's one of the reasons why change is hard. No matter how unproductive or self-defeating our habits are, if we're currently alive, then at least they haven't violated our brain's primary goal.

One way our brains keep us alive is by balancing our energy budget. Thoughts and actions all require energy, so our brain constantly makes predictions about what might be a good investment and what will likely decrease our supply.

From an energy budgeting perspective, persisting after failure is a poor use of this limited resource. You had a thought, took an action, and it didn't work. So *why on earth* would you do the same thing *again?* That seems like a guaranteed waste of precious energy!

What you and I both know, though, is that failure is an essential part of learning and growth. *Failure is feedback!* It's how we learn what works and what doesn't when we wade into unfamiliar territory.

If your brain is opposed to the very skills that lead to personal growth—persistence, grit, determination, and resilience—then it's understandable that the fear of failure has such a powerful influence on our lives.

How do we get around this so we can comfortably fail, learn, try again, and grow? Here are *two steps* to trick your brain into supporting you as you try, try again:

1. Positive outcomes are worthy of our precious energy, so consciously identify what you'll gain from your journey. The danger-monitoring parts of your brain will be taken off high alert if it's clear that the goal is worth the investment.

    If you get lost and feel discouraged, reconnect with your "why." Ask yourself, "Why am I trying this? What positive thing will persisting bring to my life?" Stay connected to the journey and the big picture. In that context, little "failures" aren't so critical.

2. *Do not* refer to negative outcomes as failures. Let's avoid that
    word so we don't trigger our brain into energy-protection
    mode.

    You tried something, and in return, you got helpful feedback.
    Now you're going to use that feedback and try something
    else. Use this type of productive language even when you're
    talking to yourself.

*Note: Productive thoughts aren't the same as "toxic positivity." Everything
isn't always "good," and we shouldn't aspire to always be happy. But
negativity is rarely productive, meaning it doesn't lead us anywhere
worth going.*

*Always allow yourself to feel your feelings. Disappointment after not
getting what you wanted is perfectly reasonable. However, wallowing in
sadness or disappointment doesn't move you forward; in that sense, it's
not "productive."*

*After experiencing a tough situation and feeling your hard feelings, ask
what would be "productive" and serve your goals and your best self. That's
the type of thinking that takes the sting out of our failures.*

HERE'S YOUR CHALLENGE FOR THE WEEK

Start paying attention to where you tend to experience "fear of
failure." We all have different insecurities, and our brains support
decisions that protect us from our vulnerable areas.

Then, make a conscious effort this week to try something uncomfortable or that you predict you might not succeed at. (*See how I avoided the "F" word?*) We're going to try to trigger that fear of failure.

Use the two steps above to help your brain tone down the warning sirens. Connect to your why and the positive outcomes you stand to gain from your actions. Reframe how you think about your outcomes.

Every time you try something scary or feel a tough feeling and the world doesn't end, you increase your "window of tolerance." This is the collection of experiences you're able to engage in without your nervous system freaking out. You felt the fear and did it anyway; you stretched the zone where you could comfortably exist. That literally creates expansion in your life.

Writing this book triggered my warning signals almost every day! The closer I got to completion, the more my brain tried to convince me to prioritize other "important" projects.

I used these two steps to let my brain know that time spent writing was a good use of my precious energy resources. Time spent on this book was time invested in a goal I had for myself. No matter what anyone else thought of the finished product, it would be a significant accomplishment for *me*.

Once my brain was back on my side, I could regain my focus and motivation and settle into my work.

Life is always easier when your brain is on your side. Learning to speak its language will help you achieve what you desire in life.

You've got this! See you next week.

NOTES

....

....

....

....

....

....

....

....

....

....

....

....

....

....

....

....

WEEK 22

Surround yourself with good energy

I HAVE A friend who can find a crisis in any situation. Whenever I talk to her, I can feel my breathing get shallow and my shoulders tighten. If I let the conversation go on too long, I even end up with a headache.

Time spent with this woman is a great illustration of the power of **co-regulation**, the process of emotionally and physically synchronizing with others. It's a powerful aspect of human interaction that impacts our emotional and physical well-being.

On a neurological level, humans are a social species. Our brains know that being part of a group increases our chance of survival, so they want us to be in sync with those around us.

Have you ever walked away from a conversation and felt baffled by what you said or how you acted? Your brain probably went on autopilot and mirrored, or co-regulated with, the other person. It's one way we're built to connect with others.

Since we're built to co-regulate physically and emotionally, the company we keep has a measurable impact on our health. Studies of people in social situations have found that co-regulation leads to synchronized breathing, heart rate, blood pressure, and hormone levels.[6]

From a survival standpoint, it's adaptive to be co-regulated with your pack. But in our modern lives, we have goals beyond just survival, and not everyone we spend time with positively impacts our mental and physical well-being.

When we engage in positive social interactions, our bodies release hormones such as oxytocin and endorphins. These "feel-good" chemicals elevate our mood and have a beneficial impact on our physical health. Reduced stress levels, lowered blood pressure, and even improved immune function are just a few of the health benefits of positive social connection.

Conversely, negative or stressful social interactions dampen our mood, raise our blood pressure, increase our respiratory rate, and trigger the release of stress hormones like cortisol.

You can't stop yourself from co-regulating with the people around you. It's a biological process that's built into you. That's why it's essential to surround yourself with people who are literally good for your health.

Let's spend this week noticing how we co-regulate with others. Pick a few people you spend a lot of time with and see if there's a pattern to how you feel around them.

If you discover people who tend to leave you feeling peaceful and happy, *find a way to spend more time with them!* Time with these people is literally good for your health!

You might also find people who leave you feeling tense and agitated. It's extreme to cut these people out of your life (although sometimes that's a reasonable decision). Recognizing how you co-regulate with them can help you decide how you'd like to interact with them.

Be careful about the time you spend with these people. Make extra effort before, during, and after interactions with them to consciously regulate your physical and emotional activation. If you don't feel up to managing your co-regulation with them, give yourself some space.

If the relationship can handle it, let the person know how they affect you. Share that their complaining, gossiping, criticizing, or judging leaves you feeling physically upset, and you don't like this feeling. Tell them you value your relationship, but when you start feeling this way, you'll take a time-out from the interaction for the sake of your health.

They might not have any idea that they impact others in this way. And they might not care. But it's a way to protect yourself from the dark side of our biological drive to co-regulate with others.

You can't change your life by changing others, but you *can* be mindful about how you interact with them. Mindfulness is one of the best tools we have to protect our peace and create the lives we want.

You've got this! See you next week.

NOTES

Expand your emotional vocabulary

WE'VE ALREADY CHATTED about the wisdom you hold in your body and the human tendency to *ignore* that wisdom as we attempt to think our way through life's challenges.

We've also discussed how our emotions don't live just in our brains; they live in our bodies, too. However, we tend to think of problems with our bodies as separate from our thoughts and emotions. We want to fix our bodies with medicines rather than listen to the signals they give us.

I remember experiencing this "confusion" at a particularly busy time in my life. One afternoon, I noticed how jittery my stomach felt. In the past, my first instinct would have been to assume I was hungry or anxious. But because I'm getting better at acknowledging my body's wisdom, I took a second to check in with myself.

A **body scan** revealed that my heart was beating rapidly, my breathing was shallow, and my shoulders were tight. Hmmm, more signs something was up that I wasn't addressing.

I shook out my shoulders and took a few slow, deep breaths to calm my nervous system. Then, I started investigating. I went through some **emotion words** to see if any resonated with me. Nervous? Dread? Resentment? Anticipation? Excitement? Frustration? Stressed? Embarrassed? Overwhelmed?

Bingo! Overwhelmed, that was it! I teased apart where that was coming from, and it wasn't surprising. It was holiday time, and I was way overextended. All of my commitments were good things, but too much of a good thing is still too much.

There wasn't an easy solution, but I knew my tendency to buckle down and do *all the things* (even if it wore me down) had been triggered. That's a habit I'm working to change, but sometimes I only notice it once I'm already in too deep.

I decided to focus on my most essential responsibilities and anything that directly served my family and drop the rest. To keep myself from feeling guilty about what I'd dropped, I reminded myself that I was mindfully *choosing* to cancel out of things, even though they were important to me, so I could better enjoy the commitments I was keeping.

When we *accurately identify* the emotion we're experiencing, we can trace its source and address it productively. Sometimes, merely acknowledging its presence allows it to move through us.

When we don't do this, we tend to assign a small set of emotions to everything we experience. The big ones we usually default to are angry, happy, and sad. That's rarely helpful and usually inaccurate. Greater nuance leads to a more effective response.

HERE'S YOUR CHALLENGE FOR THE WEEK

Luckily, there's a resource you can easily find online that can help you get more accurate at identifying your emotions. It's called an **emotion wheel**.

There are many variations, and they're all equally helpful. They expose us to more specific emotions than we tend to think of on our own.

Depending on which emotion wheel you look at, there may be over 100 different emotion words for you to play with. It's fun to read the emotion words and imagine experiencing each of these feelings.

This week, find an emotion wheel online, print it, and keep it somewhere handy. Then, when you feel physically activated, look at the wheel and see if you can identify what you're *really* feeling and what might be the cause.

After you get some experience using these precise emotion labels, see if there's a pattern to what you feel most often. For example, instead of thinking you're frequently angry, you might discover that you often feel ignored or discounted. Those are feelings you can *do* something about.

You'll feel it in your body when you land on an accurate emotion word. It's like your body is telling you, "*Yes!* That's what I've been trying to tell you!"

Honoring your truth by accurately identifying what you're feeling brings peace to your body and mind. We want to be seen and known by others, but we also desire to be validated by ourselves. Getting to know *yourself* is the key to healthy self-esteem *and* satisfying relationships with others.

You've got this! See you next week.

NOTES

Steer clear of drama triangles

HAVE YOU EVER experienced this bewildering situation? You're interacting with someone who doesn't seem *outright* hostile or negative, yet something about the situation doesn't sit right with you.

The words you hear and the body language you observe don't match up with what the person seems to be communicating. You feel manipulated, but you can't quite tell how.

This happens with people who aren't comfortable being direct. If you don't feel at ease with honest, direct communication, you end up expressing yourself subversively.

This can look like hinting, sarcasm, passive-aggression, or a variety of gaslighting techniques meant to distort your perception of reality to make it seem like *you're* the source of the problem.

It's bad enough when you experience this in conversation with *one* person, but when you have *two* people pushing you to participate in their drama, it can be hard to wrench yourself free.

An uncomfortable (and unhealthy) dynamic that occurs with three people is the "**drama triangle.**" Drama triangles are manipulative interactions that help the instigator gain power in a dysfunctional way.

Let's be clear here, though. I don't mean dysfunctional as in *bad* or *wrong*; indirect communication often gets people what they want, but it carries unintended negative consequences. There's a cost to not being authentic and honest.

When people don't feel genuinely powerful in their own lives, they might create a drama triangle to manipulate others. In their mind, this tactic is useful because it's effective in the short term. They attain what they *think* they desire in that moment.

The downside is that it leaves others feeling belittled, blamed, confused, manipulated, isolated, or attacked. None of these are hallmarks of a healthy relationship.

In a drama triangle, everyone is deceived into *believing* they have power, but since the dynamic relies on manipulation, this is an illusion.

The roles in a drama triangle are **victim, rescuer,** and **persecutor.** Here's a brief description of each role and a tip for recognizing and avoiding this dynamic.

Victim: Victims don't take responsibility for their circumstances and don't think they have the power to change their lives. They blame the *persecutor* for their situation and look to the *rescuer* to solve the problem. They get their power from manipulating the rescuer and vilifying the persecutor.

Rescuer: Rescuers try to save the *victim* from the harm being caused by the *persecutor*. They get their power from thinking they're a hero who's helping someone in need.

Persecutor: Persecutors are critical and skilled at finding fault with others. They blame *victims* for getting themselves into tough situations and criticize rescuers' attempts to help. They get their power from feeling superior to the other two roles even though they do nothing to resolve the issue.

Since I slip into an "empathetic helper" role quite easily, I'm an easy mark to be used as a *rescuer*.

I have two family members who spent decades avoiding honest, direct communication with each other. Teasing and snark were their normal modes of communication.

I hated the tension these interactions created, so I'd jump in and protect whoever was being put in (or choosing) the victim role. And when I had the good sense to steer clear, I'd be recruited by both sides to validate their perspective.

Even when I believed I *was* helping, the dynamic made me feel physically ill. It was clear I was a pawn in a drama that wasn't mine. It wasn't until I learned about drama triangles that the uncomfortable episodes made sense.

HERE'S YOUR CHALLENGE FOR THE WEEK

Even if you don't personally rely on drama triangles to claim power in your life, you'll likely get pulled into one at some point. Here's how to free yourself so you can have more authentic interactions.

The first step is to be aware of how interpersonal interactions make you feel. Anytime you feel icky inside, your body is telling you that things might not be as they seem on the surface.

Step back and look at the roles people are playing. If there's blame, helplessness, and fixing, you're in a drama triangle!

Figure out which role you've been playing, step out of this role, and try something more positive and productive.

If you've been playing the **victim**, try to identify the *outcome* you'd like rather than focusing on the *problem*, and determine the steps you can take to achieve it.

If you've been playing the **rescuer**, try encouraging the victim to connect with their *inner wisdom* and devise their *own* solution.

If you've been playing the **persecutor**, try listening to others to understand situations more deeply, partnering with them in problem-solving, and engaging in self-reflection around your own struggle with personal responsibility.

We take on different roles in different situations, but we all have one role we're most comfortable with. I mentioned that the rescuer comes easily to me. Which of these resonates most with *you?*

By understanding drama triangle dynamics, I no longer allow myself to get sucked into the rescuer role. I'm happy to support people who desire change, but I have boundaries that protect me from getting sucked into other people's drama.

We all desire to feel needed and valuable and to have the power to create the outcomes we desire. If we can help others and be helped in healthy ways, we won't need to rely on manipulation to connect with others.

You've got this! See you next week.

NOTES

Challenge your labels

AS A SOCIAL species, time spent with others usually has a positive effect on our emotional and physical health. We don't always get to choose who we spend time with, though, and some people have the opposite effect. You know who I'm talking about—the ones who are picky, critical, negative, self-centered—I could go on and on!

I bet some automatic thoughts pop into your head the second you think about people like this. You label them, and then without even realizing it, you treat these people differently based on those labels.

Once you've labeled someone, you have expectations about how they'll act when you're with them. And here's the funny thing about your brain—it doesn't like to be wrong! Once you decide how things *are*, your brain looks for evidence that you're *right* and ignores evidence that you're *wrong*.

If you don't challenge your beliefs about people, no amount of evidence to the contrary will ever change your mind. You'll no longer see people as they are; you'll only see them as you *believe* them to be.

Not seeing people as they are is a great way to kill relationships. I know I've mentioned this before, but what people want, more than anything, is to be seen for who they truly are.

A friend of mine constantly brags about *one* of her children. That child can do no wrong! She's always talking about all the wonderful things this child is up to. When she mentions her other child (which isn't often), it's only to report on that child's most recent screw-up.

It's highly unlikely that one child is *all* good and the other is *all* trouble. And even if that's true, those identities may have been influenced by the mother's labels. It's a loop that won't change until someone intentionally breaks it.

It's heartbreaking to watch someone harm their relationship with their own child because they can't see beyond their label. Luckily, there's an easy solution to keep you from falling into this trap!

HERE'S YOUR CHALLENGE FOR THE WEEK

The best way to see people as they are is to be *fully present* when you're with them.

When interacting with people this week, pull your mind into the present. Paying attention to what's happening in the moment requires mental energy and focus. When your mind is occupied in the *present*, it has fewer resources to devote to storytelling from the *past*.

You can't be thinking about how your child "*always* messes up" if you're fully focused on what they're telling you right now. You can't mentally complain about how your mom "*always* criticizes you" if you're focused on listening to her words and her intended message.

If your brain tries to jump to a label you have for this person, challenge it! Are they acting consistent with that label *right now*? If they are, inquire further:

- What *else* might explain how they're showing up?

- What *grace* could you extend to them?

- What could you *ask* them to help you better understand their behavior?

If they aren't, re-evaluate your label. It obviously only represents part of this person's identity.

When we step back and see people fully, we allow them to show up as their most authentic selves. Sometimes they *will* confirm our label, and that's okay. People aren't always going to show up as their best selves, and some have lost touch with the best version of themselves. The point is that you were open to seeing them without bias.

This week, practice being present with people and seeing who they are beyond your automatic labels. It's a gift that opens the possibility for greater connection.

You've got this! See you next week.

NOTES

Learn from the pain in personal attacks

DOES SOMEONE IN your life seem to love pushing your buttons? And be honest with yourself here, is there someone close to you whose buttons *you* love pushing?

A sad reality is that it's easiest for people to hurt those they know best. Knowing someone well presents the opportunity to effectively attack their vulnerabilities, and being one-up on someone is a cheap way to feel powerful.

It can be hard not to take these kinds of attacks personally, but they're often just a sign the attacker has pent-up negative energy that needs to be released. Lashing out takes little thought or self-control, and if people believe their friends and family will stay with them no matter what, it's low stakes to release their fury on them.

Another person's words are most painful when they land on something you're already sensitive about. If you consider yourself successful and someone calls you a failure, that'll slide right off your back. But if you *feel* like a failure, even subconsciously, this comment will feel like a dagger.

It's uncomfortable to witness these types of attacks. You probably know couples where one partner has no hesitation about publicly demeaning the other about their weight, style, or intelligence, or parents who entertain adult friends by teasing their children.

Fun joking is one thing, but when those jokes land where someone already feels insecure, the emotional pain can feel as intense as a physical injury.

When you're the target of attacks like this, if you can step back from your anger and hurt, there's actually a gift here.

When someone's words hit you hard, that's a giant flashing sign that this is an opportunity for self-discovery. Get *curious* instead of *furious.*

What is it about *this topic* that triggers you? Why is this sensitive for you? Does it uncover a hidden belief you hold about yourself? Is there shame, insecurity, or fear hiding here?

These highly emotional moments work in the other direction as well. People often attack *us* in the areas *they* feel least secure about. Knocking someone else down a rung does *not* move you up a rung.

The friend who secretly struggles with food and body image will likely comment on everyone else's eating habits. If you can let go of taking everything personally, the sting from these types of comments diminishes.

HERE'S YOUR CHALLENGE FOR THE WEEK

Pay attention to how people's words leave you feeling inside your body. (*This comes up a lot, doesn't it?*)

When you start feeling "activation" in your body, whatever that means for you (churning stomach, anxious energy, shallow breathing, tightness in your shoulders, etc.), take a deep breath and pause. Exit the interaction and go inside yourself for a moment.

Identify the subject the other person is using as their weapon. Then, go through two series of checks:

1. The first is a self-check. How do *you* feel about this topic? Is it a sensitive area? Do you hold self-doubt, insecurity, shame, self-judgment, or fear in this area? Do you know why? Where might this have come from?

   Is the pain based on a hurt that's *real*, or a *story* you've been telling yourself? When someone tells you a story enough times, you can start to believe it. It's essential to do your *own* assessment.

Either way, extend yourself some grace. If this is an area for personal growth, where can you start so you can stop feeling bad about yourself? And if the story *isn't* true, what *true* story can you tell yourself when this feeling comes up to help you shift your beliefs?

2. The second is a check about the *other* person. Might they be trying to push your buttons because this is an area of insecurity for *them*? Might their comments have nothing to do with you?

    If this seems possible, extend grace to *them*. They may be struggling with something and don't know a better way to handle it. In this case, protect yourself with a boundary, and don't take on their baggage.

When you're honest with yourself about your vulnerabilities and have grace for yourself, your triggers will fade away. Then you can see someone else's attacks for what they are—a release valve for their own negative energy.

One of the stepping-stones to peace is letting other people's issues be just that—*their* issues. Deep breaths and acknowledging their struggle can keep your nervous system from getting activated.

You've got this! See you next week.

NOTES

HALFTIME

Before we go further, let's take a moment to celebrate! You're **halfway** through your *year of personal growth*!

How do you feel? What have you learned? Have you been putting any of your new skills into practice?

Hopefully, you've begun to recognize the negative voice in your head as Anxious Mouse, and you treat him with compassion, but you don't let him hold you back.

Maybe you're also getting good at listening to your body and respecting its wisdom, celebrating the good in your life, and pulling yourself into the present.

We've also discussed humans as social creatures, the importance of relationships, and ways of interacting that protect and honor ourselves and serve our ability to connect.

Now is a great time to look over the table of contents and see if you can remember the skills that went along with the topics we've covered. Give yourself a great big "GOOD JOB!" for the ones you've tried and have led to a shift in your thoughts, feelings, and actions. Write yourself a love note reminding you of the ones that stood out but that you've forgotten.

Learning a new perspective or mindset and thinking it could make a positive difference in your life is easy. It's another thing entirely to remember to *live by* this principle. Keeping at it is the key to change. New responses are hard, but familiar responses become habits.

There's lots more to come, so when you're done celebrating, reflecting, and refreshing your memory, let's get to the second half of your year of personal growth!

Empower with your words

BY NOW, YOU'RE well on your way to noticing how situations make you feel physically and honoring the wisdom held in your body. You've likely also observed how some words can impact you both physically and emotionally.

This power hit me during a week when I had conversations with three different people who kept using the word "poor" to describe someone. Like, "Poor Sally, her life is a mess." Or "Poor Sam, he's so sick."

Each time, the word brought a sense of heaviness into my body. It felt so disempowering for the person they were describing.

After this revelation, I thought about other ways these people and their experiences could be described. When I was more specific and described their *actual* situations instead of labeling their conditions, the heaviness lifted.

"Sally's dealing with a lot right now." "Sam is very sick."

Do you feel a difference in your body when you read these different descriptions of Sally and Sam? Adding the word "poor" cast Sally and Sam as victims. Victimhood is never helpful. It communicates weakness and a lack of power.

We always have choices, and we always have power. There is always a way for us to have agency, even when our lives are filled with situations and consequences that are (seemingly) beyond our control.

We do the same thing when we have pity parties for ourselves. We might not use the word "poor" in our heads, but when we paint ourselves as victims, we lose sight of our power (*check out the Afterword to see how this showed up in my own life*).

Accepting reality for what it is and making empowered choices from that place is essential to a satisfying, authentic life.

No matter what's going on in Sally's life, those things are her reality. Feeling sorry for her does her no good. However, accepting her present situation as fact and supporting her growth going forward from there is empowering.

If you want to help Sally, don't come to her out of pity. Come to her as a partner who's prepared to share part of her load during a tough season of life.

Give yourself the same gift. After you "feel the feels" around whatever tough situation you're facing, watch how you speak to yourself. Focus on all the options that are available to help you move toward a future that feels exciting.

HERE'S YOUR CHALLENGE FOR THE WEEK

Let's practice experimenting with the power of words in both our speech and listening skills.

Notice how your own words influence how you feel. When you don't feel good inside, reflect on what you've been telling yourself. Are you using disempowering language to describe your situation? Are you caught in victimhood thinking? Can you reframe these thoughts in a more empowering way?

Try the same thing when listening to other people. If a conversation left you feeling heavy or deflated, think about the language the speaker used. What type of lens was influencing their view of the world? Did they focus on what people can't control or on all the available choices? Are they stuck lamenting the past, or can they see future possibilities?

Words are powerful. Our attitudes and mindsets are reflected in our words, and our words unconsciously influence our feelings. Auditing your language will help you feel better and open you to a more empowered way of experiencing the world.

You've got this! See you next week.

NOTES

....

....

....

....

....

....

....

....

....

....

....

....

....

....

WEEK 28

Seek out others' best selves

ONE OF THE lessons we learned during the COVID-19 pandemic was the profound impact of social interaction on mental health. We're coming to understand that connection is as much a human need as food and water.

In fact, a 2020 study from MIT found that a "hunger" for social interaction and a "hunger" for food look the same in scans of the brain.[7] The way some people show up in the world, though, can make this hard to believe.

These people need their best selves seen more than anyone! When you're miserable, hostile, or aggressive, you're often received negatively by others. This makes you feel alone and unwanted, and the misery gets amplified.

To break this cycle, step back from the interaction and ask yourself: What does this person want me to see? What am I missing?

When people grumble and complain, they often give us clues about how they want to be seen. They're telling us they feel invisible and don't know a better way to connect.

I had a client whose husband was desperate to be seen as helpful, but he didn't help in ways that were meaningful to *her*. She expressed her frustration through complaining, and his rejection was expressed as anger.

By getting in touch with his *intention*, she was able to see him differently. He felt seen when she communicated appreciation for his desire to be helpful. Then, from this happy place, he was eager to take direction about where to help.

If you can decipher someone's negativity as a clue to how they'd like to be seen, you can create connection and harmony with almost anyone.

HERE'S YOUR CHALLENGE FOR THE WEEK

When you come up against someone who is acting out, ask yourself my special question:

- How does this person want to be seen that I'm missing, and what could I say or do to let them know I see them?

If this person's inner child is having a tantrum and has riled you up, you may need to calm your nervous system before you try this strategy. When someone meets us with an attack, our natural reaction is to attack back.

Take a slow, deep breath and remind yourself that this tantrum is about something deeper than the current situation. *Then* think about what this person wants people to know about them.

Think about power, strengths, values, and needs. If they had effective communication skills, what might they share with you? What could they be craving and not receiving?

You don't need to diminish yourself so others can shine, and it's not your job to empower other people (empowerment is an inside job). You *can* be curious, though, and ask questions. This is how we let people know they matter.

The people who "see" us are very special. By helping others show up as their best adult self instead of their upset child self, we serve others, give ourselves some peace, and open channels for connection. We're contributing to the best version of humanity. That's growth to really be proud of.

You've got this! See you next week.

NOTES

WEEK 29

Manage your generosity

WHEN I BEGAN working to shift my **people-pleasing** habit (although I prefer to call it "**over-giving**"), I shared with my husband that I'd gotten overextended in the past by always being willing to take on "one more thing."

I had a history of doing this even when I could feel myself approaching burnout. My intention was well-meaning—the desire to be helpful and to lessen others' loads—but it put my needs at the bottom of the stack.

Interestingly, after I explained this, my husband shared that it never even *occurred* to him that I had been putting off my priorities when I was supporting *his* needs.

I think I had expected others to be considerate of my boundaries without me having to say anything. I thought people could sense that my plate was full and appreciated that I still made space for their needs. I had been expecting people to be mind-readers.

As I learned how to set healthy boundaries, I had to shift my beliefs about others' requests and my responsibility to myself. Changes to my calendar had to follow changes in me.

Not surprisingly, I have a *lot* of clients who are over-givers. Over-takers rarely get overcommitted because they're masters at delegation. Over-givers, on the other hand, end up burned out and resentful. They need to shift their beliefs and habits before they can change how they manage their boundaries.

To better manage commitments, over-givers need to understand these three things:

1. As long as you keep saying yes to others, they have no way of knowing when you'd really like to be saying no. They can't read your mind. They don't know what you're giving up to be there for them. Some people wouldn't care, but in many cases, if they *did* know, they'd want you to choose yourself rather than sacrifice for them.

2. You can't blame others for being over-takers if you never set boundaries with them. Some people don't have an off switch for how much they'll take, and this will wear you out if you agree to every request.

3. While you're always welcome to *choose* to be helpful, generous, and accommodating, you should only do so if the choice to give comes from your heart without an expectation about how your gift will be received. Don't do it if you're saying "yes" because you want to be valued and thanked. Helping is a gift. Be a good gift giver and don't expect something in return.

HERE'S YOUR CHALLENGE FOR THE WEEK

This week, you're going to audit the activities, responsibilities, and people who receive the precious gift of your time and energy. Then, you're going to make conscious choices about where you will and won't give this gift in the future.

To begin making these conscious choices, tap into your body's wisdom. Even when something is worthy of your time, if you don't have the bandwidth for it, your body will let you know. You'll hold tension and discomfort when you're not honoring your truth.

Look over your calendar. What commitments trigger anxiety and tension? Where does this tension live?

How did you get involved with these tasks? What about them makes you feel uncomfortable? Did you commit to them out of a sense of obligation? Is your calendar full of things you feel you "should" do?

What would you *like* to do with your time if you had more of it? What's getting crowded out of your life? Make a list. What needs and desires do these activities fulfill?

Now, commit to fitting *your* priorities into your calendar. Your priorities give you the energy to power through your other commitments.

You might have to reprioritize your activities, say "no" more often, and cancel things you've already said "yes" to. That's okay. Going forward, the goal is to say "no" (or at least "let me get back to you") when you feel your body saying, "Please, no more!" in the first place.

This is true self-care. *This* is self-love. You can fulfill your commitments with greater skill and vitality when your generosity doesn't outpace your energy.

You've got this! See you next week.

NOTES

Free yourself from past hurts

I ONCE HAD a client who, in her mid-60s, was just beginning to step into her authenticity. She felt weighed down by a lifetime of resentment toward her husband. She believed he had always dismissed her dreams in an effort to keep her content serving *his* needs at home.

When we were together I could see glimmers of her vibrant spirit, but this dark cloud of negative feelings kept her from showing up in her life as this glorious version of herself.

To begin clearing this darkness, I suggested we play around with **forgiveness**. This did *not* go over well!

Forgiveness is a sticky concept. It often rubs people the wrong way because it feels like letting someone off the hook for the hurtful thing(s) they did.

I have a very different take on forgiveness. I only work on *self*-forgiveness with my clients.

This can take some mental gymnastics to fully comprehend, but once my clients sit with the idea for a while, it's a very powerful mindset shift.

Instead of focusing on what the *other* person did to us (which makes us a victim), keeping our attention on *ourselves* is much more empowering.

We're all accountable *to* our best selves and responsible *for* our own actions. Other people's actions are not our concern. We didn't cause them, we can't change them, and it's not our responsibility to forgive them.

We owe it to ourselves to live as our authentic selves, but since this is tough to achieve, we also need to forgive ourselves for the times when we fell short.

When I asked my client if she could extend forgiveness to past versions of *herself*, she didn't understand the task. She kept repeating that *her husband* was the one who had caused the problem. She hadn't done anything wrong!

I held her hands and had her say this sentence starter out loud: "I forgive myself for..." And then the *real* pain (and tears) came flowing out:

- She was mad at herself for being "weak" and always giving in to her husband so easily.

- She felt harsh judgment toward herself for letting him treat her this way for so long.

- She regretted that she never returned to school to become a teacher, which had been her dream.

- She was ashamed that she never told anyone how unhappy she felt.

I had her imagine a younger version of herself, the woman who had experienced all these hurts. Then, I had her hold this younger woman in her heart and extend her love and compassion. She told this young woman that she knew she did the best she could at the time, and she forgave her for not acting differently.

Finally, she promised this younger version of herself that now that she was stronger and knew better, she would *do* better. She would take all the things she'd learned about herself and allow her best self to shine!

These two versions of the same woman were now partners, both dedicated to creating what they wanted for themselves going forward.

Let's practice using *self-forgiveness* to release ourselves from past hurts. Then, when new hurts pop up, we'll have experience keeping our focus on ourselves rather than on the actions of others.

Whom do you feel anger, resentment, or bitterness toward? If someone doesn't immediately pop into your mind, pay attention to who your brain complains about. Your inner monologues of complaints are your brain's way of protecting you. Anxious Mouse thinks the people who hurt you are dangerous and wants to keep you safe from them in the future.

Now, think about the version of you that this person hurt. Hold this old version of you in your heart. You might not have been able to do right by them in the past, but you will honor them going forward.

Say to yourself, "I don't know why this person acted the way they did, but, unfortunately, they weren't able to live in their light. I forgive myself for my past actions, and I release myself to live in *my* light now."

Sometimes, *we're* the ones who hurt others in the past. The same process holds in these situations. You were doing the best you could, and now you see a better way. Forgive yourself for your past actions so you can shine without guilt or shame going forward.

Making amends for how you showed up in the past will further free you from "old you" and help others heal from past hurts. If you have the opportunity to make amends, do so with humility and sincerity. Not every situation allows for direct repair, however. In those cases, your greatest act of atonement is how you choose to live going forward.

When we forgive ourselves, we acknowledge our humanity and recognize that making mistakes is a natural part of learning. It empowers us to learn from our experiences, become more resilient, and cultivate deeper self-compassion. Freed from the chains of the past, we can move forward with peace and purpose.

You've got this! See you next week.

NOTES

....

....

....

....

....

....

....

....

....

....

....

....

....

....

....

....

Build a strong pack

OUR NEED FOR social connection likely comes from deep in our primitive brain. Our brains believe there's safety in numbers and want us to be part of a pack. If our subconscious mind believes our pack membership is being threatened, we'll behave in ways that aren't always in our best interest.

Sometimes, we hold our pack members too tightly to avoid feeling abandoned. I've worked with parents who gripped onto their children and struggled to let them become independent adults.

I've also worked with people who were unhappy in their relationships but felt unable to speak up because they were afraid they'd drive the other person to leave.

Conversely, I've worked with people who *wanted* to leave their partners but feared being alone. Their Anxious Mouse convinced them that a bad partner was better than no partner.

A strong, healthy pack doesn't put too much pressure on any one member. It's made up of a collection of people who share their passions and interests in different ways.

When your pack is full and balanced, you'll feel the security that comes from connection and support. You'll know you're surrounded by the right people, and you won't feel the need to grip any one person too tightly, or fear losing people who aren't lifting you up.

HERE'S YOUR CHALLENGE FOR THE WEEK

We're going to do some art again this week!

Draw a circle on a piece of paper, and then divide that circle into six pie slices. This is your Pack Wheel. Write the following headings by the slices:

- Recreation and Relaxation

- Intellectual Stimulation

- Spirituality

- Hobbies and Creativity

- Health and Personal Care

- Personal Cheerleader

Fill each slice with the names of people who can support you in that aspect of your life. Think of people who match your level of interest and drive, share your values, and can inspire or support you.

Some people might be a good fit in more than one slice. Someone you can count on to lift you up (Personal Cheerleader) might also share your spiritual beliefs or be someone you can share fun adventures with.

However, the same person can't be your go-to person in *every* slice! That's asking too much of them and doesn't show an appreciation of where you're a really good match.

After you fill out the wheel, notice which slices have the fewest (or no) names. A full, healthy pack is one where you feel authentically connected with at least one person in each of these areas.

For the empty slices, brainstorm where you might be able to connect with people who match your interests in these areas. Examples include social clubs, sports teams, classes, networking organizations, and community groups. Then, reach out to at least one of them during the next week to find out how to get involved.

In the past few years, I've gotten involved with several volunteer organizations, started playing Pickleball, joined a Toastmasters club, a group for women business owners, a writing group, and started a social club for women. I've met lots of interesting people and added a few members to *my* pack.

Your first attempt might not lead to any meaningful connections, but take that first step! It's like dating—you might have to meet a lot of new people to find a few you really enjoy.

Your pack is out there somewhere, waiting for you to step out of your comfort zone and find them.

You've got this! See you next week.

NOTES

Release yourself from restrictive thinking

HAVE YOU COMPLETED all the challenges in this book so far? Because you really *should*. You *need to* practice all the strategies I've shared. You *have to* be your best self. You *must* care about these things.

Wow. That was obnoxious.

If that felt out of character for the way I usually speak with you, there's a reason. I just used a bunch of words I encourage my clients to be wary of.

Words like *should, must, have to,* and *need to* represent **restrictive thinking**. When you're living in a world full of musts and shoulds, you've created a very small world for yourself. You've fallen under the belief that things *must* be a certain way in order for you to be safe and in control.

It's normal to clutch onto what's familiar to us, so I would never judge a client for these restrictive beliefs. Remember, Anxious Mouse doesn't like anything new. New equals scary. Even if the past hasn't been *great*, at least it feels *familiar*. A small world can be a comforting, controllable world.

The problem with this type of thinking is that you decrease your options and possibilities when you allow your brain to fall into this habit of restriction.

There are infinite possibilities in this world! Why restrict yourself? And why judge *others* for living outside of the comfortable constraints you've placed on *yourself*?

When I'm working with a client and they use one of these restrictive words, they learn to expect that I'm going to stop them immediately and do some investigating.

Why should things be this way? *Who* said so? *Why* are other options unacceptable? *How* do you know that for sure? *What* might happen if things were different?

Curiosity shines light into the dark and helps us see what was once hidden from us.

HERE'S YOUR CHALLENGE FOR THE WEEK

Observe your thinking this week and notice how often you fall into restrictive thinking. When you notice yourself using these constraining words, stop and ask yourself this magic question:

- *What else might be possible?*

At first, *nothing* else might seem reasonable because you've been believing that things *should* be a certain way. But there's never just one right way! Ask yourself, "What else might be possible?" Challenge yourself to come up with at least three alternatives, even if those options seem ridiculous right now.

Shifting beliefs takes time because they need to thaw and soften a bit before they can change shape. But I see it happen all the time!

With practice, other possibilities will begin to seem reasonable. Eventually you'll automatically begin seeing a wider array of options where once you only saw one.

Finally, after some time, you'll be one of those people with expansive thinking. You won't get thrown when reality doesn't match your expectations because you'll be able to embrace many outcomes. You'll be able to accept life as it is and move forward from wherever you are. That's a special kind of freedom that opens you to a full, satisfying life.

You've got this! See you next week.

NOTES

Create affirmations that work

AFFIRMATIONS ARE INCREDIBLY popular in the personal growth world. Whether you flood your environment with positive statements or just make daily pronouncements to yourself, the concept seems simple enough: regularly repeat positive statements and watch your thinking (and your reality) shift.

However, when sharing the power of affirmations, many gurus miss the mark on what makes them truly effective.

Your brain is smart, so shifting your beliefs is more complicated than just speaking something into reality.

If you've tried affirmations before and quit before they "worked," you're not alone. If you could truly just repeat to yourself how you'd *like* something to be and it would magically happen, we'd all be living our best life today.

Your brain knows what you *really* believe about yourself and the world. Alarm bells go off when you create an affirmation that's too far from those beliefs. When you start lying to yourself, your brain will get defensive and fight back.

If you hate your body and start repeating, "I love my body" to yourself every morning, Anxious Mouse will want to know why you're trying to trick him. You'll end up distrusting your own thoughts, and if your brain can't trust you to be honest with yourself, you become the source of your own anxiety.

Affirmations *can* be an effective tool in **reshaping our beliefs** if we craft them in a way our brain can accept. An effective affirmation has these four qualities:

1. It's framed in the present tense, indicating it's a truth that already exists. It's not aspirational, and you don't have to work to achieve it; you just need to open yourself to it.

2. It's specific to and for *you*.

3. It evokes a positive emotion, such as strength, empowerment, clarity, self-love, self-acceptance, joy, or gratitude. You'll feel this in your body.

4. Most importantly, it's grounded in truth. It's a statement you can believe deep in your soul *right now* that also sets you on a path toward growth and transformation.

Some examples of statements that are true and that can empower you are:

- I've done hard things before, and I can use my strengths to do hard things again.

- I am grateful for the things my body does every day.

- I have the power to shape my future with my choices and my actions.

- I am worthy of deep and meaningful connections, and I open my heart to give and receive freely.

- I have the strength to be stronger than my fears.

- I am proud of who I'm becoming, and I embrace my unique journey.

- I give myself permission to heal from past hurts, live boldly in the present, and create an abundant future.

HERE'S YOUR CHALLENGE FOR THE WEEK

Try crafting a few empowering affirmations that resonate deeply with your innermost desires and aspirations.

Begin by reflecting on areas of your life where you feel you're holding yourself back, such as self-confidence, self-acceptance, connection, career, or health. Ask yourself why you haven't been thriving in the area you chose. The messages that surface are hints about your limiting beliefs.

Then, using the qualities of *effective affirmations* as your guide, compose affirmations that embody the *truth* of who you are and who you *aspire* to become. Write them down, repeat them daily with conviction and emotion, and observe how they gradually mold and shift your automatic thoughts about yourself and what you're capable of achieving.

We've spoken before about the power of your language and inner dialogue. When crafted correctly, affirmations can be a helpful tool in retraining the way you speak to yourself.

You talk to yourself more than anyone else, so you have tremendous influence over yourself. If you are your biggest cheerleader, you'll always have someone around to straighten your crown and believe in you.

You've got this! See you next week.

NOTES

WEEK 34

Learn from your shame

HOW DO YOU feel when you hear the word *shame?* It's definitely one of the ickiest feeling emotions.

We feel shame when we believe we've acted out of alignment with our true selves. If we believe we acted this way because we're flawed, bad, or broken, our shame will morph from being about what we *did* to being about who we *are.*

Our shame can also come from external sources. When someone says we should feel ashamed, they're telling us we're acting inconsistently with who *they* think we should be.

It's excruciating to deny the true self, but we face challenges to our authenticity every day. Since none of us will *always* make choices that serve our best selves, we need to know how to deal with shame.

It's natural to want to avoid thinking about our darkest parts and the moments when we let ourselves (or others) down. Nothing good ever comes from hiding from our feelings or judging ourselves for them, though, so this week, let's shine a light on one of our most painful emotions.

HERE'S YOUR CHALLENGE FOR THE WEEK

Follow these five steps to help you *use* your shame feelings to direct you toward a more authentic life. For this exercise, give yourself at least 20 minutes of uninterrupted time in a relaxing space. Start by closing your eyes and taking a few slow, deep breaths.

1. The first step might be the hardest—start by identifying and admitting to your "shame." Try sitting with the word for a while.

   Ask yourself, "Where do I feel shame? What aspects of myself and my life feel shameful? When have I acted shamefully?"

   Take your time. If your shame is well hidden, it may take a while for it to rise to the surface. Everyone has areas of their lives, though, where they wish they had shown up differently.

2. Greet this shame with kindness. One reason it was hesitant to come up is that it's usually judged harshly. Listen to your shame with compassion, treating it the same way you treat Anxious Mouse.

3. Identify how your shame betrays your *true self*. To do this, ask what *value* of yours was violated.

   If you value truth, did you lie? If you value speaking up for yourself, did you stay silent? If you value family, have you not made them a priority? If you value health, did you make choices that don't serve your body? If you value self-care, did you deny your needs? If you knew someone else's expectations didn't serve you, did you try to meet them anyway?

4. *Forgive yourself!* (Remember week 30?) Release yourself from guilt and judgment. You did the best you could at the time, given the circumstances. Now you understand where shame comes from, though, and you can honor your authentic self going forward.

5. Finally, create an action plan for *how* to do better going forward. Don't leave this to chance or good intentions. Get clear on your values. Make a Personal Values List and keep it somewhere handy.

   While you're not in the heat of the moment, ask yourself how you'd *like* to show up when each of your values is challenged. *Visualize* yourself acting this way. Help your brain know what this looks like and that you're capable of acting this way.

For example, if you have the habit of staying silent rather than challenging people, tell yourself, "When I'm in an uncomfortable situation and tempted to stay silent, I will take a slow, deep breath, identify my truth in the situation, and speak up with a statement that represents that truth. I might be met with hostility, but in the long run, being true to my best self is more important and will allow me to live at peace with myself."

When you're done, seal in the practice by reflecting back on it. What did you learn about yourself? Did your shame come up easily, or did you find some you've been protecting yourself from?

Were you consciously aware of your values, or was this the first time you clarified them to yourself?

Did mentally rehearsing a new way of showing up strengthen your confidence and connect you to your authenticity?

Hiding shame eats away at your soul. Your true self isn't always going to be perfect, but it is inherently good. By connecting to your values and doing your best to live by them, you can accept and love yourself for who you are.

You've got this! See you next week.

NOTES

WEEK 35

Keep an eye on your stories

ONE OF THE most valuable things a coach can do for their clients is help them become aware of the invisible lenses they wear to help them interpret the world. These lenses represent what we've come to believe about the world from our personal experiences.

Once the lenses are identified and removed, the client is opened to a new, more expansive view, one with choices and opportunities they hadn't been able to see before.

One way these lenses prevent us from seeing the truth is through the stories we tell ourselves.

Humans are meaning-making machines. We're constantly taking in bits of data and crafting them into stories that help us make sense of them.

In many ways, this is an adaptive strategy that serves our safety and survival. A world without patterns and predictability is a scary, confusing world. If an educated guess can protect us from danger, it's worth making the leap!

The downfall of this strategy, however, is that sometimes we create stories that aren't true. We might connect dots that aren't related to each other or fill in gaps based on what we experienced in the past.

A common feature of the faulty thinking we use to create our stories is **mindreading**. Mindreading is assuming we know other people's thoughts, motivations, and intentions. An observation and a whole lot of assumptions can create a powerful—but incorrect—story. However, once we've created our story, it can be hard to let it go.

Have you ever walked away from a group and then heard them all laughing? Since our brain wants to protect us from danger, it may create the story that everyone is laughing at us. The story's purpose was to make sense of the group's behavior and protect us from dangerous people. But that story also creates bad feelings based on assumptions we didn't bother to confirm.

A psychological principle that keeps us stuck in our stories is **confirmation bias**. Once we believe something to be true, our brain is partial to evidence that supports our story. It also filters out evidence *against* our story. This leads to a cycle of rigid thinking that reinforces our false beliefs.

Like so many things we've discussed here, the first step in releasing ourselves from our stories is to become *aware* of them. Way back in week one, we learned that the voice in our head doesn't always serve our best interest. It may be well-intentioned, but it's often hyper-focused on identifying danger.

If you've gotten this far, I hope you're beginning to listen to what you tell yourself with a critical ear. I hope you're building the habit of grounding yourself in the present. These actions will help you fact-check the difference between what you're *actually* experiencing and observing and the story you're telling yourself.

HERE'S YOUR CHALLENGE FOR THE WEEK

You've developed many new tools over the past 34 weeks, and now we're going to use some of them to free ourselves from stories that don't serve us.

Our stories have patterns based on our beliefs about ourselves and the world. As you've been listening to the automatic stories your brain creates, have you noticed any themes?

Are there specific *words* that seem to pop up frequently? *People* or *situations* that get your Anxious Mouse squeaking? Going forward, these are going to be clues that you might be in a story.

Those pesky restrictive words *always, should, must,* and *have to* are also clues that you've found a story. Our stories often describe a world that's black or white, and life is rarely like that.

The next time you hear yourself telling a story about your situation, be a reporter. Imagine you can only include things in your story that you have *evidence* for—things you actually saw and words that were actually said.

Now, notice the parts you filled in. These might be assumptions about intentions, motivations, or outcomes.

Once you've separated the things you know to be true from the parts you added, what's the *new* story? If you need more information to help you make sense of the facts, do what a reporter does and gather it! Curiosity is *always* better than making assumptions.

Challenge yourself to come up with five new ways of interpreting the situation. Do yourself a favor and try to use frameworks that hold yourself and others in a positive light.

Finally, notice how this changes your world. Does it allow you to see people differently? Does it open up new options and possibilities? Does it free you from roles you've been playing or thought you *should* be playing?

Everyone tells themselves their own stories, and these stories shape our reality. Sometimes, the first step in creating change in your life is as simple as allowing yourself to write a new story.

You've got this! See you next week.

NOTES

Manage your mental complaining

WE'VE ALREADY TALKED about the brain's natural tendency to tread into negative territory when we don't keep an eye on it. One type of internal dialogue our brains love to entertain is **mental complaining**.

Mental complaining is common when we feel like we're not in control of our lives. The complaining might be directed outwardly, such as resenting others for asking too much of us, or inwardly, such as judging ourselves for not speaking our truths.

After my oldest child graduated from high school, I felt utterly burned out on volunteering. I vowed to myself that I'd take a year off from any type of volunteer role. I might show up and be a helper for a day, but I certainly wouldn't agree to organize anything.

Then, *literally* the day after I made this promise to myself, I was offered the opportunity to run an incredible year-long project at my son's school.

I wanted to say yes so badly. But what about my promise to myself? I decided I needed a new deal that more *authentically* addressed my struggle.

If I said yes, it had to be with an open heart and a total commitment to the project's mission. If my brain started complaining when I felt overwhelmed, drained, or taken advantage of, I would remind myself of *why* I agreed to take on this role and that I made the choice *mindfully* rather than out of obligation, guilt, or fear of saying no.

Mental complaining is just another way our inner narratives can suck the joy out of life. We give away our power when we tell ourselves stories that put us at the mercy of our environment.

Being mindful of our choices and taking action when we're not happy with our situation gives us agency over our lives. When you feel a sense of control over how you're spending your time and energy, there's a lot less to complain about!

HERE'S YOUR CHALLENGE FOR THE WEEK

Notice when your mental complaining shows up. We don't start it consciously; it's one of those automatic narratives that run on autopilot in our minds when we let it.

Catch it! What's the complaining about? What patterns are you noticing? What events, situations, people, or tasks trigger your internal complaining? Is the complaining related to those good old restrictive words must, have to, or should?

Just like last week, fact-check yourself. If you're getting into situations you don't want to be in, how does this happen? What's leading you to violate your boundaries? Over-giving? Obligation? Guilt? Fear of disappointing people?

Managing your energy and your obligations is a great way to help you feel agency over your life. Use your values and purpose as your North Star, guiding decisions about what gets a share of your precious time and talents.

Then, if complaining surfaces, you can remind yourself that you *chose* this path with intention. This puts you back in the driver's seat of your life.

Connecting to your *power to choose* helps you approach commitments with a positive spirit. You're no longer going along for the ride; you are actively creating your experience. Feeling like you're the master of your life is essential for mental health.

Whether you're feeling grumpy about going to work, driving your children around, attending social engagements, or participating in volunteer activities, when you're mindfully acting out of *choice*, you can come to your commitments with a peaceful heart and a feeling of empowerment.

P.S.—In case you're wondering, I agreed to run the volunteer project, and it was one of the most fulfilling projects I've ever participated in. It was a LOT of work, but I got to know a great group of women, some of whom have become my best friends, and we created something truly memorable.

My mental complaining *did* pop up at times, but I had a clear, positive response to it, and poof, it disappeared. In its place was the beautiful reminder of *why* I had agreed to the project in the first place and all the joy it had already gifted me.

I frequently use this experience to remind *myself* of the power of mindset. A simple shift can elevate our mood, energy, and sense of power and control in our lives.

You've got this! See you next week.

NOTES

Practice nonattachment

THERE'S AN ANCIENT Chinese parable that beautifully illustrates the power of mindset. Clearly, I'm not the only one who loves this story. I come across it all the time as a teaching tool in fields such as sports, business, and parenting.

> An old farmer had worked on the land for many years. One day, his horse ran away, and upon hearing the news, his neighbors came to visit.
>
> "We're so sorry to hear this. It's such bad luck."
>
> The farmer responded, "Bad luck. Good luck. Who knows?"
>
> The next morning, the horse returned, bringing with it three other wild horses.
>
> Upon hearing the news, the neighbors returned. "What great luck!" they exclaimed.

The farmer responded, "Bad luck. Good luck. Who knows?"

The following day, the old farmer's son tried to ride one of the untamed horses, got thrown off, and broke his leg. The neighbors again came by to offer their sympathy, "We're so sorry. What bad luck…"

The farmer responded, "Bad luck. Good luck. Who knows?"

A day later, military officials came to the village to draft young men into the army. As the son's leg was broken, they passed him by. The neighbors congratulated the farmer on how lucky his son was.

The farmer responded, "Bad luck. Good luck. Who knows?"

The story demonstrates the power of the Buddhist concept of **nonattachment to self** (usually just referred to as *nonattachment*), the practice of letting go of expectations so we can experience life as it is.

You were beginning to practice nonattachment when you freed yourself from obsessive thoughts, paid attention to the way you label people, watched your use of restrictive words, and separated truth from assumptions in your mental stories.

When we feel we must label events in our lives as good or bad, lucky or unlucky, success or failure, we attach a *meaning* to these events that doesn't actually exist. Reality just *is what it is.*

Sure, it feels great when things go the way we wanted them to, and celebrating those moments adds joy to our lives. But the opposite side of the coin is that we set ourselves up to be upset or disappointed when things *don't* go as we'd hoped, even if we have no power over the outcome.

Nonattachment is *not* the same as indifference. Indifference is a lack of interest or concern. Nonattachment is accepting reality and moving forward from where you are without judgment. It's a very freeing mindset.

HERE'S YOUR CHALLENGE FOR THE WEEK

Just for fun, let's practice seeing reality for precisely what it is, without labels or values. This can be a huge mindset shift, so give yourself space to play with this idea.

Think of something in your life you would characterize as either *good* or *bad*. Now, state it as a fact without labels or emotion.

For example, "My car needs over $1000 in repairs."

This experience might make you angry, anxious, frustrated, or disappointed. Try dropping those labels and embracing reality for what it is.

Your car needs over $1000 in repairs. That's reality. This wasn't done *to* you; it just is. Cars get old and need repairs. This is reality, and it's just a neutral event.

From this place, you get to choose how you'd like to move forward.

How does this feel to you?

You can practice this mindset shift with any of your daily tasks. When you're doing regular daily activities, such as driving to work, making coffee, or doing laundry, intentionally let go of any expectations you have about how the activity *should* unfold.

Traffic may or may not happen. Either way, whatever happens is reality. The coffee might be perfect, or the machine might leak water. And the time you spend folding laundry is exactly the amount of time that task needs. There's not a "better" use of your time if that's what needs to be done at the moment.

Approach activities with a sense of curiosity and openness. Allow them to unfold naturally without trying to control the outcome.

This is a challenging practice, but releasing expectations can bring ease and freedom to our lives. When the world is always as it should be and we're free to interact with reality as we choose, we can go with the flow of life with contentment and peace.

You've got this! See you next week.

NOTES

Increase your joy with the 80/20 rule

A COMMON ISSUE that leads people to seek coaching is the feeling that they no longer enjoy their lives. Their lives have become full of *"have-tos,"* and they no longer have time for *"want-tos."*

When I help clients with this concern, some of our work is to identify what drains them. We also look at beliefs around *shoulds* and *have-tos* to identify options and choices they hadn't considered.

A principle that's helpful in this work is the 80/20 rule. The 80/20 rule states that 80% of the outcomes in life come from 20% of the actions.

This rule, also known as the *Pareto Principle*, is frequently used in business to enhance efficiency. If 80% of your success stems from

20% of your actions, savvy companies will direct resources toward identifying and nurturing that 20%.

This principle applies to joy, too! As in, 80% of the joy in your life probably comes from about 20% of your actions. Investing in that 20% will pay off in enhanced life satisfaction.

You probably can't eliminate *everything* in that 80%, but this 80/20 mindset offers a framework to help us be more mindful about how we spend our time and engage with the things we "have" to do.

HERE'S YOUR CHALLENGE FOR THE WEEK

Let's use an 80/20 list to increase the joy in our lives.

Take a piece of paper and divide it into three columns. Put "80%" at the top of the first column, "20%" at the top of the second, and "Missing" at the top of the third.

Now think about an average week. List all the things you do during your week that *don't* give you joy in the 80% column, and all the things that *do* give you joy in the 20% column (the 80% column doesn't actually have to contain 80% of your activities—we're using these percentages symbolically).

First, let's look at the 80% column. Some things will be easy to cut out of your life. If scrolling social media is a mindless habit but doesn't bring you joy, think about how you could fill that time with something from the 20% column.

When you're tempted to slide back into these habits, remind yourself that you're *choosing* to spend your time on something that doesn't bring you joy. These activities are suddenly less appealing when we're conscious of their cost.

For the tasks you really do "have to" do in your 80% column, how can you do them more efficiently? Remember that 20% of your actions lead to 80% of your results. Can you delegate tasks that aren't critical? Give yourself time limits? Break them down into manageable pieces to reduce overwhelm and procrastination?

Even just thinking about these tasks differently can keep them from diminishing your joy. What good things in your life come from doing these tasks?

Paying bills allows you to have electricity and running water in your home. Grocery shopping is an opportunity to choose the foods you get to eat. Even picking up dog poop is only a job you have to do if you have a faithful canine companion in your life!

Next, let's examine the 20% column. How could you structure your life so that 80% of your time is spent on *these* types of activities? Just becoming aware of your 80% and your 20% is a wonderful first step toward being more intentional with your time.

Finally, what brings you joy that isn't on the list at all? Those things go in the Missing column. By shrinking the time and energy you spend on your 80% column, now you'll have space for these!

By continually looking to shrink the 80% of our lives that dampen our joy and expand the 20% that challenges us, leads to growth, and fills our cup, we're always on the path to mindfully crafting a joyful life.

You've got this! See you next week.

NOTES

....

....

....

....

....

....

....

....

....

....

....

....

....

....

....

Create a "chuck it" list

I'M ASSUMING YOU'VE heard of a "bucket list." You might even have one.

A bucket list is a list of things you'd really like to do during your lifetime. It could be places you'd like to travel to, activities you'd like to try, or things you'd like to learn.

I've tried to keep my bucket list short. Realistically, being in my mid-50s, I want to focus on unique experiences that will fill me with awe and wonder.

I'm also reconsidering the level of discomfort I'm willing to endure. Seeing the Northern Lights was at the top of my bucket list for a long time. Lately though, the idea of freezing my buns off for a string of evenings without the guarantee of seeing anything is starting to seem less appealing!

A few friends and I recently shared our bucket lists. Some of these ladies have lists so long it was exhausting just to *hear* them!

I'm all about personal growth and meaningful experiences, but if *listening* to a list exhausts you, it might be time to consider a "chuck it" list.

A chuck it list includes things you once aspired to do but you're now letting go of. This doesn't mean you *won't* do these things or you no longer find them *interesting*. It just means you're accepting the idea that if they don't happen, you won't be left with regret.

A chuck it list is a way of acknowledging that time, resources, and opportunities are finite resources. We're constantly making choices in our lives. Choosing one thing doesn't make other options less important or valuable, but sometimes we need to prioritize, and that's okay. That's life.

As you make your choices and set priorities, if you never release any old dreams or goals, you can end up stressed or feeling that you've let yourself down. That's the opposite of the purpose of a bucket list!

It's completely normal to need to mourn the release of an old dream, so let yourself feel the sadness or disappointment if that comes up. But ultimately, the space this release creates will free up resources for new possibilities.

If you don't have a bucket list, start here. Be extremely clear with yourself about what type of list it is, though. Is it fun and aspirational? Like, if these opportunities came up, you'd totally do them? Or are these experiences you're committed to making happen?

If it's the latter, pick one item from the list *right now* and figure out the first step toward making this dream a reality. Fulfilling your dreams takes action and energy.

If you already *have* a bucket list, give it a refresh. What feels outdated, out of reach, or adds unneeded pressure to your life? Can you begin releasing these items?

Perhaps have a fun ceremony where you release the dream into the universe, making it available for someone else to adopt. Or replace it with something more relevant, exciting, or easily attainable.

Even if you don't have a bucket list, making a "chuck it" list can be a fun exercise. What do you release yourself from accomplishing during your lifetime? Have fun with this. Be silly!

I did this with some friends, and I released myself from climbing Mount Everest. It wasn't ever on my bucket list, but I released myself from considering the possibility all the same. And while a marathon is still on my bucket list, I released myself from participating in any 100-mile runs. That would definitely require more training than I'm interested in.

If I'm ever possessed to actually *try* one of these things, well, how lucky for me that I get to have a bonus life experience! That can make it feel even more special. But I'm not going to stress about making space in my life for goals that don't resonate deeply with me right now.

You've got this! See you next week.

NOTES

Uncover your hidden money mindset

MONEY, LIKE SEX, politics, and religion, is a sensitive topic that people avoid talking about. Clients rarely come to me because they want to work on money issues, but you'd be surprised by how many issues turn out to be *related* to money.

I've had clients improve relationships (or end them), quit smoking, lose weight, recover from burnout, reduce stress and anxiety, and reconnect to purpose, none of which *seem* related to money, but often, money mindset was a hidden part of the problem.

Once these clients dealt with their money fears, they felt freed to make big changes in their lives. Deep in their hearts, these were changes they wanted for themselves, changes they secretly knew would enhance their lives, but that they were avoiding because of their beliefs around money.

Our money mindset is shaped by a combination of factors, including our upbringing, cultural influences, past experiences, and societal norms. Often developed early in life, it can be deeply ingrained and subconscious, making it challenging to recognize its influence on our financial and life decisions.

This week, let's pull back the curtain to uncover how money influences *your* life choices. Then, we'll do a little fact-checking to help you free yourself from money-related limitations.

HERE'S YOUR CHALLENGE FOR THE WEEK

To uncover your limiting beliefs around money, ask yourself this question: What would I do if money wasn't an obstacle? If I was guaranteed that, no matter what I choose, there would be no negative financial impact?

Would you change jobs? Change careers? Quit working? Travel? Go back to school? Move? Make a big purchase? Start a business? Enter or leave a relationship? Help someone else with *their* financial needs? Start a foundation? Make a big donation?

On a scale of 1 to 10, how strongly do you desire this outcome? When you imagine experiencing it, how much does it fill your body with joy, peace, or excitement?

Now, on a scale of 1 to 10, how impossible does this outcome seem based *solely* on the financial strain it would create?

Finally, let's reality check this strain. Is it *really* money that's holding you back from your desires? Sometimes we blame our financial situation when the real issue is our sense of deservingness, fear of failure, discomfort with change, or lack of confidence about next steps.

Set aside some time to research the true costs associated with the desire you identified. Sometimes, they're not as insurmountable as we imagine they are.

If financial considerations really are an obstacle, think outside the box about this desire. Is there a "junior version" with less financial impact? A way to dip your toe in the water before deciding to take the full plunge?

What about creative ways to finance your dream? Have fun with this. The options don't all need to be realistic. You'll be surprised at the great ideas that come up when you free yourself to brainstorm without boundaries.

Now that you have a clearer vision of what you desire, the financial commitment, what else might be holding you back, and possible ways to finance your dream, you can plot a path to your desire. It might not look exactly as you'd imagined, but a shifted dream is better than a dream left to die.

You've got this! See you next week.

NOTES

Make friends with imposter syndrome

THERE'S A *HUGE* industry aimed at helping coaches and small business owners grow their practices. My inbox is *flooded* every day with marketing emails, each promising the "magic formula" for radical business success.

I rarely read them, but one time a subject line made such an outlandish promise that I *had* to open it to see what sham they were promoting. Turns out their "secret" was an attitude I'm not a fan of—*fake it till you make it.*

I know some top motivators in the personal growth space who are big fans of this strategy. There's another way of dealing with self-doubt and imposter syndrome, though, that's much more effective. It's always better to work *with* your authentic feelings than to try to "trick" yourself into feeling something else.

You're never going to "get over" imposter syndrome. Top professional athletes work with sports psychologists to manage self-doubt. CEOs turn to coaches and advisors for guidance and feedback. Top musicians and actors struggle with the fear that their most recent success will be their last.

No one ever *really* thinks they've "made it," not even the people who appear most self-confident. It's how the brain is programmed.

One of my favorite celebrity quotes about imposter syndrome is from Meryl Streep. It's said that in a 2002 interview for USA Weekend, she said, 'You think, "Why would anyone want to see me again in a movie? And I don't know how to act anyway, so why am I doing this?"'

If *Meryl Streep* hasn't conquered imposter syndrome, what hope is there for us mere mortals?

While you can't *defeat* imposter syndrome, you *can* learn to manage it effectively. The process is similar to the way we work with Anxious Mouse.

We just covered the first step—*recognizing* that self-doubt is a normal thinking habit. And as we've learned before, just because you *think* something doesn't mean you have to *believe* it.

Next, *challenge* these thoughts with your smart, rational brain. Just as professional athletes have experienced many successes to get where they are, you've had lots of successes in *your* life, too.

Remind yourself of your strengths and skills, how you've overcome difficulties in the past, and that you have what it takes to do it again.

Finally, *choose* an empowering statement that supports your growth and success. Base it on something you actually believe about yourself or the situation. Remember—your brain knows when you're lying to it.

HERE'S YOUR CHALLENGE FOR THE WEEK

The next time self-doubt creeps into your mind, instead of believing it, trying to ignore it, or aggressively shutting it down, meet it with compassion first. Make friends with your imposter syndrome! Let it know you expected it to rear its fearful head, but you're not going to let it hold you back.

Remind yourself of the strengths you possess that have helped you succeed in the past. Pump yourself up with statements that are real and true for you. If you did the "I Am" art project from week twelve, read over those qualities to reconnect with your best self.

Reclaim your nervous system so you can think clearly and show up fully. Take a few slow, deep breaths, and exhale completely, like you're blowing out a candle. Ground yourself in the present by attending to your environment. Shake out your shoulders or any other body part that's holding tension. Swaying back and forth soothes the nervous system as well.

Once you've calmed your body and affirmed your authentic power, there's no need to *fake* it because you know you've *got* it! You can feel confident showing up as you are because you know everyone experiences self-doubt and everyone has room to grow.

You're not a finished product yet, and you don't have to be. Perfection is not the goal. Do your best today, knowing that if you continue showing up, you'll improve your chances of doing even better in the future.

You've got this! See you next week.

NOTES

Protect yourself from contagious emotions

EVER SINCE THE COVID pandemic, we all know a lot more about germs and how to protect ourselves from catching them. But did you know that *emotions* are contagious, too? "Catching" someone else's emotions is another way we can communicate solidarity with others.

We've already discussed our brain's drive to ensure we're accepted and valued by our pack through automatic reactions such as physical coregulation.

It turns out that this drive can impact our behaviors as well. Without realizing it, we instinctively act in ways that help us convey that we understand others' emotional experiences. The ability to understand and share another person's feelings—empathy—is essential for bonding.

One way we do this is to mimic, or copy, their reactions. This mimicry happens unconsciously and can involve copying visible reactions (such as facial expressions, hand gestures, or body posture) or physiological responses (such as heart rate and pupil dilation).

However, these reactions can also signal to our brain that *we're* the ones experiencing these emotions. In this case, we go further than empathy and actually *feel* the emotion we're mimicking. This is called **Emotional Contagion**.

One aspect of emotional health is allowing ourselves to feel our emotions. However, since we can *catch* other people's emotions, we should also be mindful about confirming that the emotion we're feeling is actually our *own*.

It can be wonderful to catch someone else's positive emotions. Sometimes, this is exactly the boost we need when we're feeling low.

Unfortunately, negative emotions seem to be more contagious than positive ones. This can be a real problem when we end up feeling bad without knowing what's upsetting us. We often search our environment for the "source" of the bad feeling (which wasn't ours to begin with) and identify problems that don't actually exist.

Groups can easily adopt the emotional tone of an individual. Families, coworkers, and sports teams are prone to absorbing the energy of a member who expresses strong emotional reactions.

If the emotion is positive, it can enhance the group's morale and cohesiveness. Conversely, if the emotion is negative, it can foster a toxic environment, leading to impaired performance and conflict.

When you notice yourself feeling emotionally activated without a clear sense of the source, consider your recent social interactions. Were you around someone *else* who was feeling this way? Is it possible that you "caught" this feeling?

Get present and ask yourself how you're feeling about your *own* circumstances in the moment. If the source of your feeling isn't your own experience, let it go! You can be a better friend, coworker, or teammate when you're not getting sucked into other people's emotional whirlpools.

Reset your physical state with techniques we've discussed before (e.g., slow breathing, grounding in the present through your senses, or rocking back and forth). Express gratitude for something in your life right now to establish a positive mindset.

It's always better to be grounded in your own experience. Check in and let go of things your brain collects without your permission. Life can be hard enough without bearing the emotions of others. Making sure the emotions you're feeling are actually *yours* is essential to living *your* authentic life.

You've got this! See you next week.

NOTES

WEEK 43

Get comfortable disappointing others

I'VE ALREADY SHARED that I prefer the term "over-giver" to "people-pleaser." I really dislike that term. To me, people-pleasing suggests a puppy desperate to win the approval of its owner. This image doesn't resonate with the motivations that lead me to get over-involved, and it rarely sits well with my clients, either.

It's generally accepted that people-pleasers fall into this behavior because they fear disappointing others. While there's some truth to that, the same actions can stem from an authentic desire for others to be happy. And while that's beautiful, there's a tipping point where the habit of giving leads to making choices that don't serve *you*.

Over-giving can look like prioritizing other people's needs, always being flexible, taking on too much, or not speaking your truth. This gets exhausting. (Which is why these people so often seek coaching!)

Unfortunately, over-givers tend to attract over-takers in friendships and partnerships. Over-takers lack awareness of when they are taking too much and may respond immaturely when someone tries to establish boundaries with them.

While it's natural to empathize with an emotionally immature person's expression of disappointment, it's not helpful to accommodate or coddle them. Allowing them to take endlessly won't help them grow, and their struggles with responsibility, insecurity, and self-esteem aren't yours to manage.

You can love others, want them to be happy, and desire to give where you can. That's all beautiful. You can't realize *your* purpose and get *your* needs met, though, when you always prioritize the choice that serves others before yourself.

HERE'S YOUR CHALLENGE FOR THE WEEK

Let's do two things this week to get more comfortable disappointing others. First, let's get really clear about what *you* actually want. Then, let's communicate that choice in a way that honors your sanctity as a deserving individual.

When you notice yourself feeling the weight of potentially disappointing someone, ask yourself these questions:

- If I were acting based only on *my* needs, wants, and preferences, what would I do?

- If I choose to do something else, how will that make me feel?

- What's the worst thing that could happen if I disappointed this person? (*If the worst thing is that you lose them from your pack, is it really a healthy relationship?*)

- Can I manage this consequence?

- Given this information, what choice do I *consciously* and *mindfully* want to make?

You're welcome to make the choice that *doesn't* disappoint, but at least now, it will be a conscious choice and not an automatic reaction.

The second step is actually *communicating* a choice that might disappoint someone. To do that, create an "I" statement, don't apologize, and don't rationalize.

Using an "I" statement keeps the focus on *your* experience, feelings, and needs. Be clear and specific, and stick to the facts.

Save apologies for when you hurt someone. Most disappointments create sadness or discomfort but no actual harm. You might *wish* you could help, but you don't need to apologize for not helping.

Finally, keep it short and sweet without defending or rationalizing your choice. You're sharing your choice and your truth. Other people might not like your decision, but you own what's true for you.

An example of a statement that follows this template is, "I have as much on my plate as I'm comfortable with right now, so I won't be able to help you. I appreciate you thinking about me, though."

If you're normally sensitive to disappointing others, this might feel uncomfortable or selfish at first. Practice saying statements like this to yourself or to people you know will be accepting of your choice. Shifting habits and beliefs takes time and effort.

When you do "disappoint" others and the world doesn't end, you'll feel an empowering freedom and strength from being able to make choices that serve *you*.

You've got this! See you next week.

NOTES

....

....

....

....

....

....

....

....

....

....

....

....

....

....

....

....

WEEK 44

Visualize your way to success

AS A NATIVE Philadelphian, I bleed Eagles green. When they made it to the Super Bowl for the 2022 season, I took the plunge and went. It was a total bucket list experience for a huge fan.

They lost, but fans felt pretty confident that the team would make a repeat appearance in 2023. At the start of December, they were 10-1 and had the best record in the NFL. A return trip to the Super Bowl *definitely* seemed within reach.

From that week on, however, they experienced one of the all-time greatest collapses in franchise history. They finished the regular season 11-6 and lost in the wildcard round of the playoffs.

Analysts and fans were stunned. What the heck happened? Nobody could point to any one thing—or even to a few things. *Everything* seemed to go off the rails at once. When this happens, it's a good clue that the **mental aspect of sports performance** must be part of the problem.

I tell this story to illustrate that even professional athletes struggle to manage their thinking. *Knowing* the kinds of productive mental habits that allow our best selves to shine is one thing. *Practicing* these habits when the pressure's on is another.

By this point in our journey together, you know many of the same skills I teach my athlete clients. You know Anxious Mouse lives in everyone's head, and while his intention is to protect us from danger, he can hold us back if we unconditionally accept his warnings.

You know how to:

- release obsessive thoughts,

- treat yourself with compassion (even when you're not perfect),

- recognize mindsets that foster growth,

- release expectations and deal with reality,

- focus on things you can control,

- manage the fear of failure and imposter syndrome,

- ground in the present,

- reclaim your nervous system reactions,

- monitor your language and your stories, and

- free yourself from limiting thinking.

You have many of the same mental skills top athletes learn from pricey sports psychologists!

This week, we're going to work with another powerful and popular tool athletes use—**visualization**.

Visualization involves imagining ourselves experiencing the outcomes we desire. The science behind the power of this tool is fascinating.

When we vividly imagine ourselves engaged in an event, whether throwing the perfect pass or delivering a flawless presentation, the same neural pathways get activated as the ones that would fire up if we were *actually* experiencing those events. Since our brains aren't good at deciphering the difference between *imagining* having an experience and *having* it, we can "practice" an experience just by imagining it. This is habit-creation gold!

If confidence is something we earn by being successful, we can increase our confidence in ourselves by *imagining* being successful.

If comfort with a situation comes from having experiences with that situation, we can give ourselves more experiences by visualizing them.

Visualization allows us to have repetitions of success in the privacy and safety of our minds. We can practice coming up against obstacles, experiencing failure, facing disappointment, troubleshooting, persevering, and succeeding. This practice increases our chances of showing up powerfully in real life.

HERE'S YOUR CHALLENGE FOR THE WEEK

Visualization can take as much or as little time as you'd like; no one needs to know you're doing it, and it's *fun*. It should be easy to practice this skill this week.

Think of something you might experience this week that makes you a little nervous. You're going to visualize this situation so you can practice approaching it the way you'd *like* to and experiencing the results you *desire*.

A few details will help make your visualization more effective.

Settle yourself into a relaxed state. Find a comfortable seat and let your weight pull you toward the earth. Close your eyes, loosen your shoulders, and take a few long, slow, deep breaths.

When you visualize, you need to look out at the world through your eyes rather than watch yourself having an experience. You want to encounter your imagined situation just as you would in real life.

Now, set the stage. Conjure the setting for your experience and soak up all the details of your environment. Make this image as realistic as possible.

Intentionally notice your surroundings. Where are you? Who else is there? What's going on? What are you wearing? What's the temperature? What do you hear? Can you detect a smell? How are you feeling?

Once you've created a sensory-rich setting, let the imagining begin! Be your best self! Do and say the things that will lead you to your desired goals. Imagine challenges popping up and handling them with ease. Win and enjoy winning. You're literally *practicing* how to show up in this situation with confidence and competence. No one can stop you from succeeding!

Afterward, write some notes from the experience.

How did you feel in this situation? What were some challenges that came up, and how did you overcome them? What strengths and resources did you call on that contributed to your success? How did success feel? Were there any consequences from your success that you hadn't anticipated? How did you handle those?

Run through the same situation more than once to see what happens each time. Give yourself new challenges. See if the path to success is always the same or if new paths surface.

This is your (imagined) world; everyone else is just living in it.

By harnessing the power of visualization, you can prime your brain for success and unlock your full potential. It's one of the easiest tools you can develop. Have fun with it this week, and when one of these situations comes up in real life, remind yourself that you've *already* experienced this challenge and handled it masterfully.

Hopefully, the Eagles spent some time in their off-season visualizing successfully working as a team again. If you happen to know anyone on the team, make sure they get a copy of this book! I'd love for them to know I'm pulling for them and their mastery of effective mental skills.

You've got this! See you next week.

NOTES

Conquer procrastination

AVOIDANCE AND PROCRASTINATION are incredibly common experiences. We see others getting things done, and we assume they never get stuck like we do. We only see the actions they *do* take, though, not all the ones they thought about and didn't act on.

Contrary to popular belief, procrastination and avoidance *aren't* signs of laziness, weakness, or lack of motivation. Procrastination is the result of a very simple principle: the **activation energy** required to do something that's easy and pleasurable is *much* less than is required for something that's going to cause us pain.

Let's define some of these words. I use the term "activation energy" to mean the energy it takes to start doing something. It's like striking the match that will light the logs that will create the blazing fire.

While "once begun is half done" may be true, some things are *really* hard to begin.

Activities that cause us "pain" are those that trigger our fear of failure, fear of success, perfectionism anxiety, sense of overwhelm, lack of confidence, or low self-efficacy (our belief that we have the knowledge, skills, and ability to accomplish something).

Using this framework, procrastination makes sense. If our brains want us to succeed, be seen positively in the eyes of others, and use energy wisely, *of course* they'll discourage us from engaging in hard or unpleasant tasks.

Procrastination is also a reasonable response when the benefits of an action aren't clear. A lack of clear rewards, consequences, or accountability can impact motivation and keep us from starting or finishing activities.

The solution, which we'll use in our challenge this week, involves uncovering the root causes of our procrastination patterns and addressing them productively. Berating ourselves for being lazy or unmotivated is *not* the solution. As we discussed back in week fifteen, when you're at war with yourself, you can't win.

When you decrease the perceived pain and get clear on the benefits associated with a task, you'll need less activation energy to get started, and the drive to procrastinate will melt away.

HERE'S YOUR CHALLENGE FOR THE WEEK

If you're actively procrastinating something right now, work on that. If not, think about something you've had a really hard time "motivating" yourself to complete.

Imagine the task you're avoiding is on one side of a "scale of justice"—those scales with two trays hanging from a support bar—and all the reasons for avoiding the task are on the other side.

Consider these questions as you think about why the task feels painful:

- Are you intimidated by the size of the task?

- Does it feel like a giant drain on your time?

- Are you not sure how to do it?

- Does it contain elements you can't control?

- Is it something you don't enjoy?

- Does it involve skills you don't consider to be your strengths?

- Are you worried you might fail?

- Are you worried about the consequences of success?

- Do you feel resentful about having to do this task?

- Have you had a bad experience with this task or something similar in the past?

- Do you not have a clear sense of the benefits you'll experience from doing it?

This isn't an exhaustive list, but you get the idea.

Next, you need to figure out how to make the pain of *not* doing the task **greater** than the pain you anticipate experiencing from *doing* the task. Examples are:

- Imagine what you'll be missing out on.

- Soak in the pain of not showing up for yourself.

- Picture how good it will feel to have it behind you.

- Set a consequence for yourself.

Use the visualization skill you learned last week to imagine yourself doing the painful thing and having the best-case scenario pan out. Imagine it being easier, faster, and more enjoyable than you thought it would be.

Finally, use some task management strategies to make the challenge easier to face. Here are a few examples:

- Break the task into small, manageable chunks and only tackle one at a time.

- Give yourself specific goals that will be easy to achieve and a timeline for each.

- Commit to doing anything that takes less than two minutes immediately.

- Set a timer for the time the task *should* require and commit to considering yourself finished, no matter the quality of your work, when that time expires.

- Give yourself a 10-minute break after every 50 minutes of work.

- Set up rewards or incentives for meeting your goals.

- Limit distractions.

- Seek help from people who might be able to make this work easier for you.

- Enlist an accountability partner.

If you're *still* having difficulty completing the task, do what I do with my clients. Offer yourself grace and compassion, and then figure out why the pain side of the scale is still heavier. The work *will* get done when the balance tips in your favor.

Sometimes, we keep tasks on our plate that really don't need to be there. Procrastination can be a signal to examine why we're doing them in the first place. In these cases, letting go of guilt about *not* doing something is the path to peace.

When you approach procrastination with compassion and curiosity—seeking to understand the underlying pain rather than disparaging yourself—you can accomplish your goals and move toward a more productive and fulfilling life.

You've got this! See you next week.

NOTES

Open yourself to gratitude

GROCERY STORES ARE great locations for observing human behavior. In my own local "grocery store lab," I've noticed that people often respond to an expression of gratitude by deflecting it back to the giver. They say "thank you" in response to someone else's "thank you," even when that doesn't make sense. Or they minimize the expression by saying, "No worries" or "It was nothing."

Someone thanks the bagger, and the bagger thanks them back. The checker thanks a shopper, and the shopper thanks them back. Someone gets out of the way so someone else can go through the door, and you guessed it, the thank you exchange goes back and forth.

I *rarely* hear someone respond with, "You're welcome."

I'm not saying there's anything wrong with reflecting gratitude. I get it; it feels like the polite thing to do. But think about it this way for a moment. Someone's thank you was intended to express appreciation. You did something nice for them, and they wanted to acknowledge your kindness. They handed you a beautifully wrapped gratitude present, and you handed it right back. You cheated them from fully experiencing the joy that comes from giving.

You're also cheating yourself out of the good feeling that comes from *accepting* someone's gratitude. As I tell my clients, when someone pays you a compliment or offers you gratitude, *marinate in it! Soak it in!* Let it feel good to be *acknowledged* and *appreciated!* We hunger for these feelings, yet we don't savor them when they're given to us.

We all deserve to feel those good feelings when they're extended to us. This is the special sauce that fills our tank and powers us through tough times.

Try it in your head right now. Pretend someone said "thank you" to you. Now, say "thank you" in response. It's a pleasant exchange, for sure.

Next, imagine someone thanking you and you smiling as you respond with, "You're welcome." How does *that* feel? Does it feel awkward to accept gratitude? Or does it feel like you've closed the loop for this beautiful exchange?

HERE'S YOUR CHALLENGE FOR THE WEEK

This week, when someone thanks you for something, resist the impulse to immediately reflect that gratitude back to them. Instead, open your heart and let it in.

Say, "You're welcome." End of story. Allow yourself to be the hero of the moment, the recipient of someone's appreciation. Intentionally acknowledge the beauty in this exchange.

Consciously notice how this feels. Can you handle being appreciated? This might sound odd, but not everyone can. Some people feel very uncomfortable in the spotlight and seek to turn it away immediately.

It's not your job to judge whether your action was worthy of gratitude. Maybe it really *was* no big deal to you. But if it was a big deal to someone else, allow them to acknowledge you. It's a beautiful thing to open your heart and accept someone's gift of appreciation.

You've got this! See you next week.

NOTES

....
....
....
....
....
....
....
....
....
....
....
....
....
....
....
....
....

Manage frustration by adjusting expectations

IN MAJOR LEAGUE Baseball, technology is now available to make calls without the use of human umpires. This raises an interesting debate: Are umpires an essential part of the game? Or is it more important to remove human error and get more calls correct?

Part of this debate involves figuring out how many errors umpires make in a game. A study by Boston University found that during the 2018 season, umpires made an average of 14 poor calls on pitches per game, or 1.6 per inning.[8]

My son is a pitcher, and strong mental skills are *essential* for pitchers. You're up on that mound all alone—all eyes are on you and the batter at the start of every at-bat in the game. It's easy to let your **mental chatter** get the best of you if you don't have strategies to control your thoughts.

It's common to see pitchers get worked up when calls don't go their way. Part of that is just the theater of baseball, but getting activated every time something doesn't go your way makes it *impossible* to consistently perform at your highest level.

When I saw the stat about the number of missed calls per game, a light bulb went off in my head. If pitchers shifted their perspective and *expected* 14 bad calls per game, they could avoid getting emotionally activated with each missed call.

I suggested this strategy to my son. Even if he threw a perfect third strike, the batter stood at the plate watching as the ball whizzed by, and the umpire called it a ball, could he say to himself, *"Well, there's one of the missed calls?"*

Using this mindset, you're telling yourself that your reality *is* aligned with your expectations. You *knew* there would be some bad calls, and this was one of them.

(Also keep in mind that sometimes you're the *beneficiary* of bad calls. Score one for the pitcher!)

Reality's failure to match our expectations is the source of most of our disappointment and frustration. We get so committed to things *needing* to be a certain way (*our* way) that we lose sight of the difference between what we can and can't control. Then, when things don't turn out the way we want, we resist accepting reality and make ourselves miserable.

When my clients complain that their spouse, boss, or children "always" do a certain thing, I say, "How lovely that they're showing up exactly the way you'd expect them to! Does this *actually* create a problem, or is it just not what you'd prefer?"

If it creates a problem, my next question is, "How would *you* like to show up differently in this situation? Because *they're* not the ones working with a coach to address their unhappiness."

We can't change reality; we can only make choices about the things that are under our control. One of the things we *can* control is mindfully examining our expectations and shifting them so we can tolerate a wider set of outcomes.

HERE'S YOUR CHALLENGE FOR THE WEEK

Is there something or someone in your life that frequently triggers you and creates disappointment, frustration, anger, or hurt? Let's apply this mindset shift here.

What's the *expectation* you're holding onto that's behind these negative feelings? What did you expect to happen, and why?

Experiment with shifting your expectations. What if you *expected* some of these interactions to go differently from how you'd *like* them to go? Would that cause an actual problem? Could you open yourself to the possibility that a wider set of options are okay?

If so, you've just created space in your life for more peace and acceptance. If not, decide what *you* need to do to set boundaries and consequences for when your expectations aren't met.

You can loosen your grip on your expectations and still aim high, get your wants and needs met, and take action to get what you want in life. Identify the places where *you* have control over the outcome and put your energy and effort *there*.

And the rest? Celebrate when things go your way and expect that this won't always be the case. This sets you up to be better equipped to let go and move on. Your energy is far too precious to be burned up in actions that don't serve you and places that don't move you forward.

You've got this! See you next week.

NOTES

Sneak past your inner critic

MANAGING YOUR SELF-TALK about yourself is a popular theme in the self-improvement industry. You've probably seen posts, mugs, notebooks, etc., with sayings like "Talk to yourself the way you'd talk to a friend" or "Be kind to yourself."

Shifting your self-talk is easier said than done, however, and now that you're *48 weeks* into your personal growth journey with me, I bet you know why!

The self-monitoring part of your brain sees safety in being liked, valued, and included, so it wants you to be perfect. It expects that you'll always do your best, say the right thing, and make people happy. When one of those things doesn't happen, it berates us like a critical parent.

- *"You're so dumb; why on earth did you tell your boss his idea wouldn't work?"*

- *"I'm so weak; why did I eat the cake when I'm trying to lose weight?"*

- *"I can't believe I said yes to that; I'm the worst parent ever."*

We're tough on ourselves both when the stakes are high *and* when they're insignificant. "Critical parent" is our brain's (negative) way of getting us to do better or fit in. Creating a positive, nurturing self-talk habit takes intention and effort.

When we do our Anxious Mouse work, we're really working on our self-talk. We're creating some space between our real selves and this voice so it doesn't seem so personal. Then, we meet it with compassion, fact-check its opinion, and consciously make a choice that serves us. Essentially, we're interfering with our automatic impulse to self-monitor and self-judge.

Here's another fun way to circumvent this well-meaning but critical voice: When we talk to ourselves, we usually refer to ourselves as "I."

- *"Am I ready for this?"*

- *"What should I do?"*

- *"I can't do this!"*

When we talk to ourselves using "I," we're using an "**inside view**." The inside view limits our thinking because it's directed by what's comfortable and familiar to us. It's based on what we *believe* to be true right now, and our beliefs are shaped by our experiences.

"Am I ready for this?" could trigger Anxious Mouse because it stirs up our fears and insecurities. If we have to ask, the answer is probably *no*! No, we're obviously *not* ready because we have some doubts. If we're not sure, we should stay away to avoid possible failure.

However, if you substitute the word "you" or your name for "I," now you're using an "**outside view**." With an outside view, it's like *someone else* is having a conversation with you. This is called **distanced self-talk**.

The outside view invites your brain to consider a wider selection of possibilities. It's like hiring a consultant to monitor your thoughts and offer an outside perspective.

"Are *you* ready for this?" or "Is *Linda* ready for this?" invites an authentic conversation with your true self. It gives you some distance from yourself. It allows you to be the outsider who's been asked to share their opinion.

This distance has been shown to enhance problem-solving, decision-making, and rational thinking, and decrease information overload, emotional reactivity, and risk perception. It helps people view difficult situations as *challenges* rather than *threats*.

HERE'S YOUR CHALLENGE FOR THE WEEK

Think of something you're feeling insecure about or an area where you have some self-doubt.

Is there something you'd like to try? A hard conversation that needs to be had? For me, writing a book brought up a lot of these internal struggles.

"Who am I to write a book? Why would anyone buy a book I wrote? I don't have any writing experience or skill. I should stick to what I'm good at." To counteract these doubts and fears, I've had many conversations with myself using *distanced self-talk* to challenge the places where my self-doubt lives.

I like to talk to myself with my name; it feels more powerful and personal to me. When I ask myself why anyone would buy a book *Linda* wrote or why *Linda* thinks she's qualified to write a book, I'm suddenly able to defend *Linda* fiercely.

This is a conversation between my fear self and my best self, and my best self is well acquainted with my strengths, talents, experiences, education, and skills (if I need a reminder, I look at my sun from week twelve).

This version of me thinks it's a shame for anyone's light to be kept hidden, including *mine*. It gives me the same consideration it would give other people.

When I do this often enough, I feel more closely connected to my strengths because I've been *reminding* myself of them. I feel more in touch with my own truth. When I ask *Linda* what she wants, it's funny how quickly "she" is able to respond.

Finally, when I catch myself ruminating over past experiences, telling myself stories full of "I" statements ("I should have..." or "Why didn't I..."), I stop myself and play with third-person self-talk.

It's much easier to have compassion for myself when that compassion feels like it's coming from someone else. Instead of berating myself for things I can't change, my best self can appreciate my journey and how much I've learned and grown. Linda did the best she could, and now Linda can do even better.

You are far more capable than your inner critic gives you credit for. Practice sneaking past that critic this week, and a whole new world of opportunities will feel possible.

You've got this! See you next week.

NOTES

Give yourself a break

I ONCE HAD a client who was a go-getter her entire life. She had always been a hard worker and a top achiever. After working for the top firms in her field, she started her own company, which, not surprisingly, was extremely successful.

When we started working together, she was burned out and ready to slow down. She sold her company but wasn't ready to retire, so she started working for a smaller firm. The work didn't take up as much of her life as working for a big firm or running her own company, but it wasn't the "right" fit for her either.

Every week, she'd share her frustration over not knowing what she wanted for her next step. And every time we identified something that fit what she *thought* she wanted, she couldn't commit.

She created the analogy of a marble collection to represent her time and energy. For decades, all her marbles had been distributed among her various work responsibilities. Since selling her company, she had reclaimed some marbles from her work life and reallocated them to her health, social life, and family. Best of all, she felt like she still had a few left in her pocket!

All the options and positions that sounded attractive would have required her to use up those extra marbles, which felt terrible. She recognized how much she needed her new, slower pace, and she wasn't ready to give that up yet.

Her experience isn't unusual. I've worked with many clients who were experiencing the physical effects of burnout. They knew their pace wasn't sustainable but didn't know how to change. They feared losing all they had achieved if they took their foot off the pedal even for a moment. To help these clients give themselves permission to slow down, I developed the model of "**seasons of growth**" and "**seasons of presence**."

Seasons of growth are like spring and summer in a garden, full of energy and activity. Seasons of presence are like fall and winter in a garden, a time to step back, rest, reflect, and recharge. True self-care is knowing which season you're in at any moment and allowing yourself to cycle between these seasons to protect your health, energy, and vitality.

Sadly, this is often easier said than done. Modern Western society doesn't value seasons of presence. We're expected to go-go-go all the time. We love words like hustle, grind, grit, and drive. We're competitive and results-oriented. Any time you're not striving for results, someone else is gaining on you.

Pushing through when we need to recharge, though, impacts our ability to perform at our best. The part of our brain where reasoning occurs doesn't function well when we're overwhelmed. No matter how hard we try, our reasoning and creativity won't be at their best when we're worn down, distracted, or stressed.

The antidote to *grind culture* is listening to our inner voice. When we connect with our truth, we know when we have the energy to go hard and when we need space to regroup. The answer is in us if we're willing to listen.

HERE'S YOUR CHALLENGE FOR THE WEEK

First, let's check in with your comfort level around seasons of growth and presence. How did the idea sit with you as you read about seasons of presence? If you're addicted to the grind, you may think slowing down for a season is loser talk, a sign of weakness or laziness.

If this resonates with you, I challenge you to investigate this belief. Where might you have acquired it? How do you know it to be true? How does it feel in your body when you power through busy, difficult, or emotional seasons? Is your belief in the need for constant productivity and growth in line with your other values?

Next, let's practice tuning into your inner experience. This week, when you find yourself busy, distracted, exhausted, frantic, irritable, or uninspired, pause and listen to your inner self. Close your eyes, put your hands over your chest, and imagine the *best self* inside of you that you drew back in week twelve. Ask it, "Are you up for a season of growth, or would you like a season of presence?"

If your best self is up for a season of growth, go for it! But if your best self vulnerably asks for a season of presence, think about what that could look like.

A season of presence might be as simple as canceling your evening plans and reading for pleasure. It might be a cry to admit that you need some bigger changes, though.

Periodically checking in with yourself is a great practice to ensure you're getting the balance we *all* need in our lives. Seasons of presence help us restore our energy, connect with our creativity, reflect on our big picture, and mindfully design our journey. Then, refreshed and recharged, we can show up at full strength for our season of growth.

Whatever season you're in, give yourself permission to embrace it fully without judgment or guilt. And remember, every season has its purpose, so trust in the wisdom of your own rhythms and let yourself bloom in your own time.

You've got this! See you next week.

NOTES

Tame your worry monster

ONE OF MY friends is a professional-level worrier. She carries the weight of the world on her shoulders. She worries about every possible potential danger for her children, my children, all the children she knows, all of her friends, her family, etc.

Needless to say, she's often very stressed and sad. Whenever I see her, I give her a long hug to try to co-regulate some peace into her nervous system.

Worry is anxiety about potential future problems. It often takes the form of "what if" questions based on **cognitive distortions**—thinking patterns that make challenges seem more threatening than they really are. Some categories of cognitive distortions are all-or-nothing thinking, catastrophizing, overgeneralizing, and rigid beliefs. Some examples are:

- What if my child doesn't get into college?

- What if there's traffic and I'm late?

- What if no one at the party talks to me?

Worrying is like rehearsing worst-case scenarios in our minds. Our brains don't always distinguish between real and imagined threats, so these mental catastrophes trigger the same stress responses as actual danger—racing heart, restlessness, muscle tension, and trouble focusing.

In true emergencies, these responses help us react quickly, but when the danger is only in our heads, they just drain our energy and cloud our thinking.

This week, we're going to replace the habit of worrying with a more productive reaction to potential danger.

HERE'S YOUR CHALLENGE FOR THE WEEK

Be on the lookout for worry-thoughts this week. When you notice one, try these five steps. They're designed to get your body and mind back under your control.

1. Breath! As you just read, there are a host of negative physiological consequences that go hand-in-hand with worry. To reset your nervous system so you can return to a calm

state of mind, the best place to start is always slow, deep, intentional breathing.

There are lots of "formal" breathing techniques you can use, but the main point is to slow your breathing, fill your belly, and be intentional about exhaling fully. After a few rounds, your body will transition out of fight-or-flight and into rest-and-digest—the state that's best for clear thinking.

2. Identify the fear. If you're *worried* about something, there's a *fear* in there.

    You may have to play around with this step for a while. Your first thoughts might be more about outcomes than fears. For example, if you're worried about a big presentation you're giving soon, you don't actually fear the presentation. Getting more specific, you probably don't fear forgetting what to say, either.

    Your *core fear* is deeper, such as looking foolish and losing respect, relationships, or opportunities, and the consequences of those losses.

3. Play best-case/worst-case/probable-case. Run through the worst-case outcome in your head. Will even the worst case really lead to what you fear?

    Then, consider the best-case scenario. What if everything goes perfectly? Are you prepared to welcome positive outcomes into your life?

Finally, figure out the probable outcome. It's probably somewhere between the best-case and the worst-case. How would you handle *that*? And how does this scenario relate to what you fear?

4. Do a control check. Considering what you've discovered about your fears and some likely *real* outcomes, what parts of this situation are in your control versus out of your control? Any energy you put toward things out of your control is wasted. You're always welcome to take this path, but nothing productive can come from it.

5. Take action! With respect to what's in your control, identify *three small actions* you can take to increase the chance that things will turn out the way you'd like.

   When you take action, even if things don't turn out the way you'd hoped, your brain knows you made an effort. It feels good to know you're an active creator of your experience. This helps keep you out of victim mode and prevents your fears from ruling your life. These are healthy, positive outcomes no matter what situation you're facing!

It's wise to expect the best and prepare for the worst, but burning up energy in worry helps nothing. Practice these steps to tame your worry monster and save the tough feelings for when bad things *actually* happen.

You've got this! See you next week.

NOTES

Take a fresh look at your environment

HUMANS ARE INHERENTLY lazy. I don't mean that in a bad way, though. Just as water seeks the path of least resistance, a healthy brain knows it's important to monitor energy and conserve it where possible.

This is why it's so important to design your environment mindfully. When you first set up your home or office, you probably prioritized style over designs that promoted healthy habits. Or you weren't intentional at all and planned to fine-tune the arrangement once you were settled.

How many spaces in your home have you meant to change, arrange, update, clean out, decorate, etc., but have gotten in a *rut* using as-is?

If you want to develop and sustain healthy habits, your environment needs to be arranged to make these habits as *easy* as possible. The path of *least resistance* needs to be the path you *desire*.

Imagine you're someone who's already living the way you'd *like* to be living. What might *their* environment be like? Now, create *that!*

If you find that every day seems to slip by without physical exercise, put your sneakers or your gym bag where you'll see them over and over again.

If you're trying to do more cooking and less eating out, leave some pans and recipes on your counter and stock your pantry with useful ingredients.

If you want to develop the habit of morning journaling, leave the journal on your sink or by your coffee maker every night so you can't miss it in the morning.

If you're trying to replace a self-defeating personal belief with one that's true and in service of your best self, write that belief on a sticky note and slap it in the center of your bathroom mirror.

I have clients place sticky note reminders all around their homes to remind them of the new habits they're trying to develop. The path of least resistance is to keep doing what you're doing right now. The more energy you put into creating a new path now, the less energy it will eventually take to sustain it.

HERE'S YOUR CHALLENGE FOR THE WEEK

This week, do an audit of your environment. From the perspective of an outsider, walk around your house, office, and anywhere else you spend a significant amount of time and ask what your environment says about you.

If I walked into your house, what predictions could I make about the way you're living? Is your home neat or disorganized? How prominent is technology? What's in your refrigerator?

How about your closet? Is it full of clothing for an aspirational life? Sizes that don't fit anymore? Clothes for a job you don't have? Workout clothes that aren't getting used? Too much stuff in general? Or is your closet arranged in a way that's consistent with how you're *actually* living your life?

Once you've assessed your environment, decide on *one thing* you will change *this week* to shift your environment into greater alignment with the life and habits you desire.

If you're not intentional about shaping your environment, it will shape you in ways you might not be happy about. But when you consciously shape your environment, it's much easier to show up as your best self. It becomes the path of least resistance. And making things easy is the best way to make sure actions happen!

You've got this! See you next week.

NOTES

Blaze a brand-new trail

CONGRATULATIONS! YOU MADE it to the *last week* of your year of personal growth challenges, so this week we're going to *go big* and really shake things up! We're going to propel you into your *next* 52 weeks with an amazing new goal to keep life exciting and vibrant.

Take a deep breath, shake out your shoulders, and get ready to apply all of your new tools to create something *special* in your life.

If you follow personal growth influencers or you've read some of the best sellers in the genre, the term "1%" probably means something to you. One percent is a very popular goal for daily personal growth. It's meant to be inspiring because it seems easily attainable.

If your goal is 1% daily growth, you only have to shift *one small thing* each day. Maybe drink a little more water or walk a few minutes longer. Perhaps spend a little less time on your phone and a little more time outside. Over time, you'll be able to look back and see how these small shifts added up to a noticeable change.

To be clear, I'm not against this idea of striving to be a little better every day. Most of the time, slow and steady is the best kind of growth. Every challenge in this book was meant to be something you could achieve in just one week.

No matter what their goal is, I always have my clients start slow and steady. The first thing we do is identify the "very first, itty-bitty, tiniest, bite-sized step" that will begin the journey to the change they desire. We do that to ensure the first step will get done in a timely manner, and to emphasize that no matter how big a goal is, you figure out the "how" one step at a time.

Sometimes, though, you're up for a *drastic* change. You crave something *big* and *new*. You no longer have the patience for slow and steady. In these cases, you need a brand-new strategy, not a bunch of small, linear shifts.

What got you here won't get you there. One-percent changes shift the *direction* of your path, but sometimes, you need to blaze a brand-new trail.

That can be scary! So, how do you tackle *that* kind of change?

Let's try it this week!

Pick something you'd like to be *totally* different in your life. It doesn't have to be big, like moving to a new country or changing careers. (Although it could be!) Use this phrase to help you think of something: "I'd like to be someone who..."

Maybe you don't just want to be able to close your dresser drawers, you want to be someone with a carefully curated wardrobe of incredible clothing. Or you don't just want to increase your physical activity, you want to become a yoga instructor.

Next, reverse-engineer the path to this big goal. Ask yourself, "What does someone who *already* lives like this do? How do they live? What does the destination look like?" Immerse yourself in this vision, just as we did when we tried visualization.

Getting from here to there might require a *major* restructuring of part of your life. But again, you don't get massive change without considerable effort. Think of this as fun, like looking forward to an awesome vacation. At the end of this journey, you'll have something amazing, and the journey itself will be full of exciting new experiences!

Like a tree, you're always either growing or dying. This will definitely inject some growth and vitality into your life.

The very first step on this brand-new trail you're blazing will *still* be itty-bitty, tiny, and bite-sized, but it will be something *completely* new. It's leading you to a 100% change rather than 1%!

You've done this before! You went 100% when you transitioned from crawling to walking and from babbling to talking. You left your old way of being behind and vaulted into a new way of showing up in the world, one that opened you to the possibility of novel experiences and opportunities.

You have the power to create that kind of shift in your life again. Pick something aspirational, identify the first step, and ignite your 100% transformation.

You've got this! See you next week.

NOTES

BONUS WEEK

Make a plan for the *next* 52 weeks

YOU MADE IT! For 52 weeks—a *full year*—you tried challenges designed to help you connect with your essence, shift your mindsets, improve your relationships, and develop habits that promote joyful, peaceful living.

Now, I'd like to offer you a *bonus challenge* as a reward for consistently showing up for yourself. Let's wrap up with another fun project that will get you thinking and leave you with a physical reminder of what you want out of life.

No matter what today's date is, since you just finished a 52-week commitment, today is the start of a new year for you. *Happy New Year!*

At the beginning of every new year, every organization under the sun—news organizations, influencers, lifestyle brands, interior designers, wellness experts, etc.—offers an "in-and-out" list of trends.

These lists are often fun. They might speak the truth (e.g., ending dumb trends), or offer helpful suggestions (e.g., new places to travel). However, there's not a single in-and-out list produced by anyone else that's ever going to be as good as the one we're about to discuss—because this one will be created *by you, for you*!

I came up with this activity one January after reading about my 10th in-and-out list of the week. I'd made a list on my phone of some of the "ins" I'd read that I wanted to incorporate into my life, but I found myself tweaking the ideas to fit my own tastes and interests. Then it struck me—why not just start from scratch and make a list that fully represented *me*?

I did a "future pacing" activity in which I imagined myself at the end of the year, feeling really good about what I'd added to my life and what I'd eliminated. I recorded those ideas and then turned them into a list, matching up the additions and deletions.

Here are a few of the ideas I came up with:

In	Out
More protein from beans and legumes.	Relying on powders and bars for protein.
Home cooking.	Fast-casual take-out.
Intentional, slow, deep breaths.	Shallow breathing with tense shoulders.
Creating fun events.	Waiting to be invited to fun events.
Wearing things because I love them.	Wearing things because they fit.
Responding to others from my calm nervous system.	Getting caught up in others' emotional energy.

While reflecting on my fantastic, imagined year, I considered categories like joyfulness, diet, fitness, relationships, career, and purpose. I thought about what each category would look like if I felt good about it, and what I'd need to change to get there.

HERE'S YOUR CHALLENGE FOR THE WEEK

Make *your* in-and-out list for the next 52 weeks!

The in-and-out pair framework is perfect for habit change because you need to change your status quo to make room for anything new in your life. And getting rid of a habit without replacing it with something new creates a vortex. If you don't intentionally fill that vortex, you'll slide back into old patterns.

First, think of things that you've discovered *don't* serve your wants, needs, desires, and values. These are "outs." For each out, identify what you'd like to be experiencing *instead*. These are the paired "ins."

Next, brainstorm in the opposite direction. Think of things you want more of in your life (ins) and what you'll need to change to have them (outs).

Finally, put this list where you'll see it daily to remind you of your desire for yourself over the *next* 52 weeks. Creating new habits takes intentional energy until they catch hold. But if you stick with them, they'll eventually become your *new* status quo.

You've got this!

xo ~
Linda

NOTES

AFTERWORD

Literally the day I finished this manuscript and emailed it to my editor, I received an interesting email of my own. The results were back from some testing I had as part of a comprehensive physical with a new primary care doctor, and the doctor wanted to talk to me immediately.

While the diagnostics hadn't been focused on my lungs, they happened to pick up a dark spot on my right lung. To make a long story short, I had stage 1B lung cancer.

I'm not someone you would have expected to have lung cancer. I was in my mid-fifties at the time and did everything that studies indicate contributes to a long, healthy life.

I was physically active, never smoked, ate a mostly plant-based diet, kept up with preventative health, had strong, positive relationships with family and friends, and kept my stress levels low. And, as you now know from reading this book, I put time and effort into learning about and adopting healthy mental practices and mindsets.

What I now know is that non-smoking women aged 20-49 are the second most at-risk population for lung cancer after smokers.

While incidences of breast and lung cancer are similar in American women, lung cancer kills 40% more women each year. Since lung cancer often has no symptoms (and, when present, are often misdiagnosed) and we don't preventatively scan for it, lung cancer often isn't caught until it's already stage 4 and has metastasized.

Everything I've shared on these pages took on a deeper meaning for me after my diagnosis. Every strategy and mindset shift became essential as I faced the uncertainties of treatment and recovery. The skills I've invited you to explore helped me stay positive, grounded, resilient, and hopeful through countless appointments and tough days.

Because I had already done the work, I was able to accept my reality, focus on the good, embrace gratitude, direct my energy toward things I could control, and find joy in small victories. When you do the work to establish a foundation of healthy mental practices, you're prepared when challenges arise.

I'm thriving right now, partly because my cancer is under control and partly because I choose to thrive no matter what I'm facing. I sacrificed one lobe of my right lung to the cancer monster, but a few months after surgery, I was back to running and testing my limits.

I've experienced firsthand the power of the practices and mindsets in this book, and my doctors have validated that their patients' mental and emotional states significantly impact their health and recovery outcomes. This isn't a bunch of fluff; it really can make the difference between life and death.

Life has a way of surprising us, and I believe that with the right mindset, we can face those surprises with courage, strength, and peace. Thank you for joining me on this journey, and may you continue to unlock your best self long after you've finished this book.

LET'S STAY IN TOUCH!

Congratulations on completing this 52—I mean *53*—week journey of personal growth! I hope these challenges have inspired you to make positive changes and to continue evolving into the best, most authentic version of yourself.

To keep the momentum going, I invite you to stay connected with me through my websites, newsletter, and social media channels. Here, you can find access to a wealth of free personal growth resources, updates on my latest projects, and information about new book releases.

Visit My Websites:
https://www.ultimateyou-coaching.com/
https://www.lindakneidinger.com

Connect on Social Media:
Instagram: @ultimateyoucoaching
Facebook: @ultimateyoucoaching

Thank you for allowing me to be part of your personal growth journey. Remember, the key to lasting change is maintaining a connection to your true self, showing up consistently, and embracing the journey. Keep challenging yourself, stay curious, and never stop growing.

Wishing you continued success and fulfillment,

Linda

REFERENCES

1. de Vries, L. P., Baselmans, B. M., & Bartels, M. (2020). Smartphone-based ecological momentary assessment of well-being: A systematic review and recommendations for Future Studies. Journal of Happiness Studies, 22(5), 2361–2408. *https://doi.org/10.1007/s10902-020-00324-7*

2. Lepp, A., Li, J., Barkley, J. E., & Salehi-Esfahani, S. (2015). Exploring the relationships between college students' cell phone use, personality and leisure. Computers in Human Behavior, 43, 210–219. *https://doi.org/10.1016/j.chb.2014.11.006*

3. Emmons, R. A., & McCullough, M. E. (2003). Counting blessings versus burdens: An experimental investigation of gratitude and subjective well-being in daily life. *Journal of Personality and Social Psychology, 84(2)*, 377–389. *https://doi.org/10.1037/0022-3514.84.2.377*

4. Hazan, C., & Shaver, P. (1987). Romantic love conceptualized as an attachment process. *Journal of Personality and Social Psychology, 52(3)*, 511–524. *https://doi.org/10.1037//0022-3514.52.3.511*

5. Werner, A. M., Tibubos, A. N., Rohrmann, S., & Reiss, N. (2019). The clinical trait self-criticism and its relation to psychopathology: A systematic review—update. *Journal of Affective Disorders, 246*, 530–547. *https://doi.org/10.1016/j.jad.2018.12.069*

6. Zee, K. S., & Bolger, N. (2023). Physiological coregulation during social support discussions. *Emotion, 23*(3), 825–843. *https://doi.org/10.1037/emo0001107*

7. Tomova, L., Wang, K. L., Thompson, T., Matthews, G. A., Takahashi, A., Tye, K. M., & Saxe, R. (2020). Acute social isolation evokes midbrain craving responses similar to hunger. *Nature Neuroscience, 23*(12), 1597–1605. *https://doi.org/10.1038/s41593-020-00742-z*

8. Williams, M. T. (2019, April 8). MLB umpires missed 34,294 pitch calls in 2018. time for robo-umps?. Boston University. *https://www.bu.edu/articles/2019/mlb-umpires-strike-zone-accuracy*

ACKNOWLEDGMENTS

Heaps and heaps of thanks to Karen Quigley, my writing accountability partner. Without our weekly check-ins, I'm sure I never would have finished this book. It also didn't hurt that you're a licensed therapist and certified coach. I've enjoyed our intellectual conversations and appreciated your occasional "coaching supervision."

I'd also like to acknowledge my editor, Dawn Thomas-Cameron. As this is my first venture into publishing, handing over my "baby" was scary. Maybe it never gets easier. In addition to your editing prowess, your encouragement was absolute gold. I still wasn't sure I could do this until you told me the book was "awesome" and that you found value in the challenges. You pushed when I needed to be pushed and gave me grace when I was down on my progress. I sure got lucky when I found you!

My friends, clients, and newsletter readers give me the kind of positive reinforcement I aspire to give others. Thank you! You're less biased than my family, so when you tell me that I help you make your life better, that means the world to me. Thank you for boosting me up when *my* Anxious Mouse tries to dim my light and fill me with self-doubt.

Someday, I'll drop off free copies of this book to all the baristas and hotel front desk managers at the coffee shops and hotel lobbies I've worked in over the past year. I sometimes refer to these places as my "satellite offices." Thank you for the warm welcomes, big smiles, camaraderie, and hospitality.

Finally, my family. I am SO lucky to have parents, siblings, children, and a husband who reflect back to me a potential I don't always see in myself. I'm blessed to be showered in love from all directions by this crew. I NEVER would have tried a book if you hadn't all thought a book was a completely reasonable idea. And now here it is—*a book*!

Life is easier when you know you have a whole team of people on your side, there to celebrate your wins, hold you up when you need support, and share the in-between times. I can only aspire to give as much as I get from all of you. Thank you. I love and appreciate you all so much!

ABOUT THE AUTHOR

Growing up on the East Coast, Linda's early experiences in sports set her on the path to her current career. As a high school tennis player, she recognized that she had greater difficulty with mindset than with athletic skill. This led her to pursue an undergraduate degree in Neuroscience from the University of Pennsylvania and master's degrees in Experimental Psychology (Georgia Institute of Technology) and School Psychology (Temple University).

Over the past thirty years, Linda's career has encompassed various roles related to psychology, personal development, and empowerment through mental skills. She has assisted individuals through her work as a school psychologist, sports coach, parent educator, volunteer coordinator, and currently as a certified coach.

Linda is the founder of Ultimate You Life & Health Coaching. She provides one-on-one coaching and workshops for organizations, businesses, and sports teams. She specializes in helping people manage life transitions and access peak mental performance. She also mentors college students and athletes in developing healthy mental habits and aids organizations with interpersonal and cultural issues.

Linda resides in Southern California with her husband and two dogs. She has two grown children who are on their own journeys to unlock their best selves. In her free time, she travels, reads, is physically active, and makes time to nurture her social connections.

www.ingramcontent.com/pod-product-compliance
Lightning Source LLC
Chambersburg PA
CBHW051507120626
46551CB00012B/813